You will be blessed by Cat[…]
soul to open to Love in he[…]
of Cathy's personal spiritual direction journey and teaching her readers
the distinctives of spiritual direction. Walk With Me *will be a wonderful*
companion and ongoing resource for spiritual growth and transformation.

Susan Vander Woude, MDiv.
Spiritual Director, Co-Founder and Partner, SoulStream Community

Don't read this book, rather take and eat of its wisdom, it's deep invita-
tion to authenticity and integration toward wholeness. Walk with it, and
then practice being sacred presence as you receive the unveiling of the life of
the other. For this privileged path is holy ground.

Doreen D. Kostynuik, M.Ed. Counselling
Spiritual Director, Part-time Byzantine Hermit

As her title suggests, Cathy Hardy's Walk With Me *invites the reader on*
a journey into presence. Words like tenderness, humility, gentleness, and
acceptance appear frequently and characterize the book's tone as well, as
Cathy teaches us to befriend our soul and to see ourselves and each other
through the eyes of love. Her empathic heart, generous spirit, and vibrant
imagination permeate the book, all in loving service to the sacred mystery
of every human soul and life itself.

Dr. Marlene A. Schiwy,
author of *Gypsy Fugue: An Archetypal Memoir*, and
A Voice of Her Own: Women and the Journal Writing Journey
www.marleneschiwy.com

Walk With Me *is a beautiful invitation to all who read this book: an invitation to a deeper, richer experience of Love. Cathy has produced an outstanding guide, combining her own spiritual direction experiences with solid teaching of the important principles in walking alongside another. Thank you, Cathy, not only for this book, but for the healing you've facilitated for so many.*

Elsie Goerzen, Coordinator, End Abuse Program,
Mennonite Central Committee, BC

Cathy is an inspiration to us. She drinks from deep wells and selflessly helps others to do the same. Everything you read on these pages comes from years of saying yes to transformation. Cathy shares her personal discoveries freely, making the trail easier for us to follow.

Steve and Evy Klassen, Founders of the MARK Centre
https://www.markcentre.org/

In Walk with Me *Cathy Hardy has crafted an invaluable resource that will allow for people to explore and recall their deepest longings and their true selves. With beautiful invitation, story and a rich tapestry of practices and reflections Cathy calls both seekers and those companioning to a place of growth and discovery that allows for significant and meaningful depth of connection to both self and the Divine.*

Gillian Drader MA RCC BCN
Trauma Therapist, Spiritual Director

When Cathy Hardy talks about the art of Spiritual Direction she describes a relationship of mid-wifing the soul, where each person is held in love, enabling that soul to emerge and flourish in all of its original beauty. Cathy has walked this path herself and she knows how to accompany others on the journey. I highly recommend Cathy and this book for those who are ready for this essential adventure.

Allen Proctor, Director of the Haden Institute
www.hadeninstitute.com

WALK
with me

**Transformation through the
Pathway of Spiritual Direction**

Cathy AJ Hardy

◆ FriesenPress

Suite 300 - 990 Fort St
Victoria, BC, V8V 3K2
Canada

www.friesenpress.com

ISBN
978-1-5255-8400-8 (Hardcover)
978-1-5255-8401-5 (Paperback)
978-1-5255-8402-2 (eBook)

1. BODY, MIND & SPIRIT, HEALING, PRAYER & SPIRITUAL

Distributed to the trade by The Ingram Book Company

Table of Contents

Our vocation does not arise from others' expectations of us.
It is a vitality that, once freed, flows out from within us;
something that our heart yearns to express in the world.
This vitality or life form becomes our legacy,
one precious day at a time.

Cathy AJ Hardy

Foreword

From the time I was a teenager, I was fascinated with transformation. Why did some people stay the way they did? What led others to change? Why were some people happy? Why were some people sad? Why did some pursue their dreams, and why did some seem frozen in time? I pondered as I observed the multi-generations of my family, friends, and the community around me. At nineteen, as I walked down the road toward a youth meeting, I was aware that I was really angry. This surprised me greatly, as I saw myself as a good girl—and *good girls* don't get angry. But I *knew* in that moment that I was very angry. I was fascinated and perplexed at the situation I found myself in. I was used to observing others. Now I observed myself. What would I do with the realization that perhaps I was more complicated than I knew? What would I do when I discovered I had negative characteristics as well as positive ones?

I realized I could shut that awareness off, or I could become curious about it. I allowed curiosity to emerge, turning toward my first *shadow*, as the great psychologist Carl Jung would have named it. I was turning toward an aspect of my subconscious that had been concealed and was now being brought into the light. Little did I know that this movement of "turning toward" was the beginning of a lifetime of learning about turning toward what was hidden, shadowy, and dark in myself—leading me eventually to growth and vitality. Little did I know that this movement would lead me toward learning about and experiencing transformation again and again.

Twelve years later, when I was thirty-one, I found myself in crisis. Someone suggested Spiritual Direction might be helpful; however, I didn't even know what they were talking about. I began to ask around if anyone knew what Spiritual Direction was and how one would find a Spiritual Director. I had many confusing conversations, as most people I spoke with had no idea about this sacred art of companionship. But eventually, one person did, and she handed me the business card of a woman named Joy.

Joy became my first Spiritual Director, and in the years following my time with her, I called her the midwife of my soul. I saw her once a month for a period of three years—three years that were incredibly formative for my life. Transformation was a slow by-product of this new journey I had embarked on, but I didn't know that for a long, long time. After those precious years with Joy, I moved across the continent back to my home in British Columbia, Canada, where I sought a new spiritual companion. Eventually I met Doreen, whom I have been with for over a dozen years and continue to see to this day.

Spiritual Direction became a deeply important aspect of my commitment to integrity, growth, and formation. I realized that this practice of going monthly to someone I trusted offered a place of accountability, facing my shadows, inner growth, and deepening prayer. Through good times and bad, this spiritual practice became a rhythm in my life that I dedicated myself to.

Over many years of receiving Spiritual Direction and through a process of discernment, I recognized that Spiritual Direction was more than something I would like to receive. It was a vocational path that my heart was guiding me to pursue. I had been offering Soul Care Retreats for over ten years and many people were asking for spiritual formation beyond a retreat experience. I was still on my own healing journey and hadn't felt ready to offer more, but eventually the day came when I knew I wanted to step into this path fully.

I pursued the training to become a Spiritual Director through the Haden Institute in Niagara Falls, Ontario. As much as I learned about Spiritual Direction from my training, the deepest learnings came through Joy and Doreen's modelling of the art of spiritual companionship, my failures and struggles as I learned to listen to others, and the precious moments of grace I received time and time again on this path of transformation. In the chapters ahead, I'd like to share in a simple way some of my learnings.

I look back at that nineteen-year-old girl, and I'm glad she had the courage to begin this transformation journey, even though she didn't know where it would lead her.

Please note that all personal stories are used with permission, however names have been changed in order to protect privacy.

With Love, Cathy

Transformation

I breathe in the sky
I breathe out
I breathe in the light
I breathe out
I breathe in the trees
I breathe out
I breathe in the field
I breathe out
I breathe in the rocks
I breathe out
I breathe in the river flow
I breathe out
I breathe in LIFE
I breathe out transformation[1]

1   Cathy AJ Hardy, Love Breathes with Me (Victoria: FriesenPress, 2018), 7

Introduction

Spiritual Direction has been and continues to be one of the greatest gifts I've ever received in my life. It's also one of the greatest gifts I've ever have had the privilege to give. Some gifts are special only in the moment, but others seem to unpack themselves forever, becoming deeply cherished with time. Spiritual Direction is a gift that continues to give; it's more valuable, precious, and rich than I could possibly express. I hold it in such high regard and treasure the sacredness and beauty of it. Sometimes I can't see the treasure of all that is happening in the moment, but over time, it reveals its great worth. Spiritual Direction is like an archeological dig in which, together, we are carefully opening the earth to find lost treasure. We may find an imprint or a shard of bone. What we discover may look like nothing of significance, but in the end, this fragment of the past could shed light on the story of our lives, opening the door to the healing of our soul.

For a long time, I had struggled to find a voice teacher who could help me where I felt stuck, and then I stumbled upon a book one day that changed my life. This book came with two CDs, which I listened to over and over. Through this person's guidance, my voice began to grow and change. I was forever grateful that the author had taken the time to write and record; however, he expressed great reservation about publishing the book, as some things can only be imparted in person because each individual singer is unique. Something transpires between the teacher and student that is significant to that person's journey. That's how I feel about writing this book for you. I hope this text can be a guide, an inspiration, an accompaniment to the treasure and richness of Spiritual Direction. But the real way to learn about

Spiritual Direction is through experiencing it yourself, receiving it over a long period of time, and letting it do a work in your life.

To fully understand Spiritual Direction, or to consider accompanying others in this sacred art, we must learn to sit in the chair of receiving. We must face ourselves and become a friend of our own soul. A document called *Vows to My Dear Heart* is the place we begin with the Soul Care Circles I lead and guide. It's about turning toward one's own heart and listening, honouring, and cherishing one's own soul. Many of us have betrayed ourselves. We haven't listened to our inner knowing, so we find ourselves deeply disconnected from our true selves, our truth, our soul. Spiritual Direction can be a gift to light the way back home through the forest of our lives. The mystics of many traditions would agree that as we come back to our souls, we come home to Inner Wisdom, Divine Love, the Source of our being, the Ground of All. We are invited to return home, to the place of our origin, the place of our wholeness, the place of knowing who we are in Love.

My spiritual roots are in the Christian tradition, and the mystics of that tradition would say that coming home to our souls is where we discover both our true selves and union with Love, the Living Presence, the Cosmic Christ, the Eternal. Far from being a self-centred pursuit, no matter what spiritual path you're on, this inner soul journey is where we face our shadows and those things that are dishonouring to the truth of our being. This path requires great courage and truth-telling. We're invited into a deeper story, the story beyond being a victim or blaming another for our suffering, the story of our soul. To actually live from the true self (our soul) is our place of greatest vulnerability and greatest courage. Those who have studied myths and legends would say that we are on a hero's journey, this journey of the soul. We will have to face all sorts of monsters and perils, but if we stay faithful to the task, we'll find our greatest treasure—the rich and wondrous diamond soul that is within each human being.

To enter Spiritual Direction is not for the faint of heart. It's a long, labyrinth-like journey. Sometimes it may feel as though we're walking in circles, but it's more like a deep walk to our roots, to the centre of our being, the place where we know we're held in love and cherished fully. As we know this place deep within our being, we can begin to live from the *inside out*. Instead of looking for validation from our accomplishments, relationships, or knowledge, we come to *rest in just being*. Instead of fearing rejection because of our failures, losses, and insecurities, we *know* our intrinsic value *just because we are*.

From this place of knowing our value and worth, we're energized to live a life of overflowing love and service. This journey, this Spiritual Direction journey, is one for a lifetime. It's not a degree to receive or a task to accomplish. It's a walk. If you dare, I invite you to *walk with me* through this writing and with a Spiritual Companion you can meet with face to face. And if this walk catches your heart, you may desire to walk with others who are desiring to join you in the way of the soul. If so, my hope is that this book can be like a friend along the path.

As I come from the Christian mystical tradition, I will write about Spiritual Direction through that lens, inspired by the life of Jesus, who invited us to access and live from the Living Water within each one of us. However, I hope my language can be broad and inclusive enough that you can find resonance no matter how you might identify yourself in terms of a spiritual tradition. As Richard Wagamese says: "I am merely one who has trudged the same path many of this human family has—the path of the seeker, called forward by a yearning I have not always understood."[2]

I believe that Spiritual Direction is deeper than any religious words you may find here. It's about walking each other home to the truth, beauty, and essence of our souls. I believe there's a mystery that we touch in Spiritual Direction that is eternal and beautiful. Some would

----

2   Richard Wagamese, One Drum (Madeira Park: Douglas and McIntyre, 2013), 27.

say this is the beauty of the soul. Some would say that we are touching the Presence of God. Some would say that it's the union of the two. I find it hard to define exactly what is going on! That's why I appreciate the mystics. They were more aware of mystery than concrete definitions of the ineffable. But I will say that when I'm aware of the mystery within us, I often use the word Love. Traditionally, the word for this is God; however, the word I most commonly use for "God" is "Love," which comes out of my experience of prayer.

Chapter I

Listening

When I first arrived for Spiritual Direction, I was in crisis. Whenever I'd been in crisis before, I'd looked for someone to rescue me. Save me. Tell me what to do. Joy didn't do any of those things, and it drove me crazy. Instead of rescuing me, Joy *listened*. She listened deeply and then she would enter a deep silence. The silence was long. So long! Sometimes twenty minutes of silence. I would feel like I was crawling out of my skin. Eventually, she told me this: "Cathy, I'm listening to the words you're saying, the words you're not saying, and to the One who loves you more."

Love in the Listening

Oh! I was so surprised. I was astounded to realize how much *love* was in the listening. Joy restrained her own personal reaction to my situation and, entering a state of the heart where she heard my words, she listened underneath my words to what was hidden. Then she did a third listening—listening to Spirit, to Wisdom ... to One who loved me more than she did.

That shocked me.

Joy was able to hold my words in a way that didn't rattle her. She opened up her intelligence to listen with wisdom, insight, and intuition. And then she opened her heart to a great listening—a listening to Love. And she trusted. How she trusted! She trusted in the One who loved me. This still brings tears to my eyes.

I realized during those precious three years that I had never been loved like that before—loved enough to be listened to *beyond* what I knew of my own situation. In such a profound way, this changed my life. This listening ultimately gave me a sense of my value, dignity, and worth. It revealed that my life was precious. The gift of being listened to helped me to *revere my own life* in a way I had never done before. I would say that this listening eventually birthed my soul. It birthed the truth of my being so that I could be born ... again ... into myself ... through the eyes of Love.

I believe this re-birth is possible not only for me, but for all who truly experience the gift of this depth of listening. I believe that this kind of listening from the soul in the Spiritual Director opens up the heart of the directee in ways that are transformative. The soul receives a great gift when witnessed with such utter love and care.

To become a listener myself has been an enormous journey. To listen as a Spiritual Director has been one of the greatest gifts and the greatest challenges of my life. Over and over, Joy's words have come back to me: "Listen to the words being spoken. Listen to the words not being spoken. Listen to the mystery of Love holding the other."

Three Kinds of Listening

Attentive Listening

The kind of listening that Joy modelled impacted my life in numerous ways and became instructive on how to listen to others. The first lesson was to grow in awareness of attentiveness. *Am I really paying attention with my whole heart and mind? Am I fully present? Listen, Cathy! Listen!* Sometimes I catch my mind taking off in another direction if something the directee says triggers a memory or idea—off my brain goes on an adventure somewhere else. *Come back; come back! Stay attentive!* This attentiveness is a discipline, an intention, a way of the heart. Sometimes people talk in confusing patterns that aren't easy to follow. *Stay attentive!* I never know when the moment will happen where certain words give a cue that this is the place of pausing and going deeper. These words are like *hot spots* and can be doorways, openings to the soul journey. Sometimes people's words are heavy with grief or fraught with anxiety. Whatever is shared, I am called to *stay attentive, be present, notice, and listen.*

> *Stay Attentive.*
> *Be Present.*
> *Notice and Listen.*

Listening beneath the Words in Silence

Secondly, this kind of listening taught me to grow in awareness of what is beneath the words spoken. One must access the intuition of the heart to listen in this way. What are the moods, the emotions, the nuances in the expressed dialogue? Where is there hidden anxiety, fear, or a covered-over thought? What was almost said, but not? What mystery did that statement hint at? What bitterness lay under that tone? What grief has not been explored? This awareness is less tangible, but one can hone the skill. This awareness of what is *under the spoken text* leads to the art of asking questions that may open doors to unmarked territory in another's soul. It is here that curiosity, wonder, and adventure lie.

> *"Listen to the words being spoken.*
> *Listen to the words not being spoken.*
> *Listen to the mystery of Love holding the other."*

As we receive the words of others, we as Spiritual Directors are invited to hold their words in spacious hospitality. We take time to pause and allow a stillness to envelop what has been spoken. There are often various "voices of self" that have been expressed, parts that are conscious and parts that remain unconscious. The silence helps us to sift past the obvious issues at hand and be attentive to the subtleties of the inner journey. Silence helps us listen beyond our first instinctive response and be attentive to questions that may arise within to guide the conversation further.

The silence helps us to sift past the obvious issues at hand and be attentive to the subtleties of the inner journey.

Silence helps us listen beyond our first instinctive response and be attentive to questions that may arise within to guide the conversation further.

Listening with Love

Thirdly, this kind of listening brought a sense of accompaniment. I wasn't listening alone. Love, the Mystery of Presence, loved this person *much* more than I ever could. I could call for help. I could call for wisdom. I could call for a path of discernment as I listened.

I always have little reminders beside me as I listen to others: icons, stones, etc. These tactile elements remind me that there is a greater Wisdom in the room. Love will guide me as I listen, and I am not alone. This sustains me and strengthens me. I can easily fall apart when I begin to take responsibility for others' lives (my weakness). As Spiritual Directors, we're not responsible for people's spiritual lives. We're meant to walk beside; to point the way, to love.

Our journey is to continue to listen to our own souls and hearts and to Love who is the Great Friend of our souls.

"But if we are willing to walk quietly into the woods and sit silently for an hour or two at the base of a tree, the creature we are waiting for may well emerge, and out of the corner of an eye we will catch a glimpse of the precious wildness we seek."[3]

Parker J. Palmer

---

3   Parker J. Palmer, Let Your Life Speak (San Fransisco: Jossey-Bass Inc.), 7

Chapter II

Rhythms

As a musician, I am impacted greatly by the rhythm of music that I listen to. It can call me to stillness, to dance, to wildness, and to many other modes of being. Rhythm is an incredible metaphor for how we live our lives. In music, there are endless kinds of rhythms—sets of numbers that create a feeling in the body. As I child, I learned that the time signature in music was for counting a linear set of beats. As a seasoned musician, I understood that the time signature means so much more; it's a sensation in the body about how a song should flow. For example, a rhythm of three beats in a song creates a feeling of swinging, swaying, or being in a waltz dance. A song with two beats makes one feel like they're in a marching band! A song with six can feel like a lullaby, or a gentle sort of swinging. When a song lacks rhythmic flow, one can't engage well in the music, as it's difficult to understand what's going on. There's a feeling of confusion and disorientation. I've come to appreciate what rhythm can do to a whole crowd, uniting us in a beat, or how it can unite a person *with themselves*, helping them come home to their truth.

I've discovered the blessing of rhythms in how I live life, both in receiving ongoing spiritual support and in being a person who offers that support to others. I don't think we can live well in this kind of work when we're scattered and full of unhealthy chaos.

Here are some helpful ways to maintain the rhythm of our lives:

Rhythm of Receiving Spiritual Care

The rhythm of spiritual care, engaging in the monthly flow of Spiritual Direction and other forms of spiritual support, can offer us as caregivers a necessary touchstone each month. What if receiving nurture for our own souls was the beginning of the musical bar, the first beat of each measure? Receiving spiritual care each month can help us see the landscape of our lives and notice the other rhythms that may be on or off. Pausing monthly is like tuning one string of our instrument. It can give motivation to tune the other strings of our lives as well. Receiving Spiritual Direction over the long haul guides us into that process of continued transformation and wholeness.

As Spiritual Directors, I believe this is something we need to commit ourselves to with our whole hearts: the art of receiving care in our own lives. This places us in a position of humility, of openness, and of continual learning. I'm continually surprised at how many people in caregiving professions are isolated. The nature of our work can cause isolation in that we're not free to disclose the vulnerabilities of our own hearts with those we're caring for. We need to intentionally set up space for our own nurture. There's always room for growth and more awareness as caregivers. Life also brings the unexpected into our lives. Having a companion to walk with helps us journey through the ebb and flow of our stories. Having safe places to disclose our hearts is a gift we give to ourselves.

Rhythm of Care for Mind, Body, Emotions

As we are present to others, we need to have clear minds, calm bodies, and steady emotions. We are invited to work with aliveness from our three centres of intelligence. When we're filled with our own anxiety, tension, and disorder, we're not able to clear the necessary space for another soul. *Soul work needs much open space—space of the inner and outer self.* To create open space, we're invited to keep our inner minds, hearts, and bodies free of toxic waste, distractions, and addictions.

Rhythms of the Mind

What nourishes your mind? What leads you back into wholeness of thought? What do you do when you're anxious? Our culture is constantly luring us with more information, more distractions, and more clutter. *Rhythms of stillness and silence lead the mind to rest.* Rhythms of letting go of obsessive thoughts create space for receiving and attentiveness. Turning our minds to Love's intentions aligns us with a deeper reality than our first reaction upon waking up. Our thought life is a place where we can encounter the Presence of Love. It's a place of facing our fears and acknowledging our anxieties. If we don't turn toward our tangled thoughts, our mental life seeds our addictions, masks, and denial.

What do you do when you're tangled? Confused? Overburdened? What are your regular thoughts? What are your temptations? What are your distractions? What if you concentrated your thoughts on truth? What if you devoted yourself to memorizing a poem, a piece of scripture, or a mantra that can guide your mind in times of stress or distraction? We're invited to create a sanctuary in our minds, a sanctuary of thoughts based in the reality of our diamond soul.

We're invited to create a sanctuary in our minds.
A sanctuary of thoughts
based in the reality
of our diamond soul.

As you accompany others, you will be impacted by all of *their* thoughts, *their* addictions, and *their* obsessions. If we're not aware of our own thought life, we can easily get hooked and tangled in another's. Our thought life needs to be rooted in truth, love, and mercy. Rhythms of the day when we focus on our thoughts are powerful in bringing us into alignment with Love.

Some practices that help clear the mind are: being out in nature, starting the day in silence, being aware of your body through stretching, journaling the Prayer of Examen, and taking time to listen to Love's guidance. Later in this book, I'll guide you into some specific journaling prayer meditations that have been extremely helpful in guiding myself and others into clearer thoughts when we've lost our way.

Rhythms of the Body

What nourishes your body? What rhythms restore your physical sense of wellbeing? The Enneagram is a helpful tool for knowing one's strength and weaknesses. As a four with a five wing on the Enneagram, I tend to thrive in my inner life. My body? Well, can't it just come along for the ride? I'm realizing as I age that I can't take this dear body for granted. I'm learning that my body needs a lot of water, it needs to move, and it thrives on schedule, rhythms, and nutritious food. This has all become part of my spiritual practice: the art of nurturing my body as a sacred task. So, as I drink my water, it's prayer. As I stretch, it's prayer. I thank my body for all it's doing to support this beautiful life, and I'm seeking to listen to the body's messages to me. Some of these messages are: Stop! Sleep! Play! Dance! Create!

Working in the kitchen, sweeping the floor, creating a meaningful working space have become part of the tapestry of nurturing the body and creating a life of soul awareness. Instead of menial tasks being a drudgery, they're part of a healthy way of life that supports the work of listening and being attentive and mindful. Everything becomes connected with integrity and faithfulness to the soul.

Many of us are deeply disconnected from our bodies, but our bodies store another way of knowing. When we slow down our bodies, we connect with our souls. Robert Sardello says: "The soul requires duration of time ... rich, thick, deep, velvety time ... and it thrives on rhythm. Soul can't be hurried or harried..."[4] What if we gave our bodies permission for rich, thick, deep, velvety time? Time to slow down, time to listen to what our bodies need? Time to listen? Time to play?

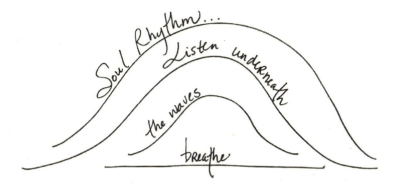

Rhythms of the Heart

What are your emotional rhythms? Are you on a roller coaster, taken by every emotional wave of the day? Are you flat-lining and not feeling anything? As Spiritual Directors, we will encounter a lot of emotions in others that rise and fall. If we're not engaging with our own emotional wellness, we won't be well equipped to navigate the wild storms of another. We must practise the art of turning toward *all* of our emotions, allowing and processing them where necessary. We've been taught to feel a great deal of shame regarding certain emotional expressions or feelings in the wider culture. It's imperative that we look at the shame we may carry in ourselves regarding emotions and the expression of emotions.

Not only must we learn to turn toward our emotions, but we must learn how to embrace them and let them guide us toward truth—a greater truth in Love. Our emotions are there for a reason, and

....

4   Tracy Friesen, Ride the Waves (Bloomington: Balboa Press, 2014), 245

although they may be childish or immature, we must pay attention to them for the healing of our own souls. These places in us can be layered very deep if they're not dealt with and may explode in a wild storm under stress.

Developing rhythms of emotional care is significant to our own well-being as Spiritual Directors/caregivers. Having an Anam Cara (the Celtic understanding of a soul friend) is necessary in our lives. We need places not only of soul care but of mutual and loving friendship. Friendships are a ground on which we can explore and name our emotions and be held and loved in life-giving and sustaining ways.

Rhythms of Friendship

One of my dear friends has walked with me through life since grade eight. We've shared a lot, as we both married in the same year and had children at the same time. My life changed greatly when I walked through a divorce and let go of how I thought my life would turn out. Evy welcomed me to express the truth of my being over and over without changing me. She welcomed me when I was weak and when I was strong. She held me when I was broken, rubbed my feet when my heart was in pieces, and cheered me on when I found my voice once again. Evy has been a gift of significant friendship as I have journeyed through life. In turn, I listen to her as she listens to me. It's a place of mutuality and respect.

My heart is full of gratitude for the gifts of friendship in my life, as I used to take them for granted and didn't realize how important they were for wellbeing and health. These are the people we will share our memories with. These are the people we celebrate with. These are the people we cry with. We need friends! We need companions! We need those who see us without title, without role, without demand. The rhythm of time with a friend is one of the most significant gifts we can receive as we move into love and care for others in service.

Rhythm of Prayer/Meditation

What is your rhythm of prayer and/or meditation? What kind of prayers connect you with the Infinite? What are your practices, and how do they flow with your day? As people offering soul companionship to others, it's important to find our rhythms of prayer and to keep returning to the wellspring within so that our cup is restored with Living Water. We all live in households with different demands, so what may work for some may not work for others. But staying with a practice for a season (e.g. a three-month period) can be helpful in finding a rhythm of prayer.

One of my favourite ways to pray each day is with the Ignatian Prayer of Examen through journaling. I write in large letters: *Consolation.* I express my heart through words all that has brought me life that day. What was life-giving? What was I thankful for? Where did I notice myself being energized? Where did I lose a sense of time? Where did I experience wonder? Then I write: *Desolation.* I fully express my fears, disappointments, anxieties, and anything else that pulled me away from my centre, the place of being rooted and grounded. I allow myself to be fully honest with my confusion, anger, angst, or pain. Finally, I write: *Words of Life.* (This part of the Examen is my own personal process that I've added to this ancient prayer practice.) I become silent and take time to listen for inner wisdom. I write what I feel Love is speaking to me. This part of the prayer has been life-changing. Love enters both my consolation and desolation and guides me into truth, creating awareness, insight, and invitations to respond to. This prayer has brought a profound rhythm into my life, and perhaps it may be a gift to you.

There are many ways of developing attentiveness to inner wisdom, and many ways to prayer. The important thing is to fall into awareness of that practice *daily* and pursue it with all your heart. This is your source! This is your life! You can't do this alone. You need to nurture this relationship with the ineffable. It's the sap of your tree. It's everything. Open your heart. *Listen and receive.* In prayer, you will become aware of the Living Presence. By knowing this Presence, you will be transformed.

In prayer,
you will become aware of the Living Presence.
By knowing this Presence,
you will be transformed.

Rhythm of Schedule

What daily, weekly, monthly, quarterly, and annual rhythms do you need for wellbeing? When do you take time out for your own personal retreat? For listening? For play? For relationships? These decisions to honour our time are sacred, and they serve those we are listening to. When we're flowing with the rhythms that feed our souls, we're more equipped to be present and attentive.

I was on an eight-day silent retreat when I realized how my whole body felt so happy when I was moving a little more slowly, especially in the early morning. Not rushing and giving myself space to go at a slow pace while doing the simple things, like dressing and savouring morning coffee, was a tremendous gift for the rest of the day. It's now part of my daily rhythm to allow time in the morning. No emails, texts, or phone calls until after 9:00 a.m. This daily rhythm sets the tone for the day. It's a time when I am able to hold the day before me in silence and take care of some of the simple things.

Ponder...
What helps me thrive on a daily basis?
What helps me thrive on a weekly/monthly/quarterly/annual basis?
What do I need to place in my schedule to help honour my life?

Jesus is an incredible model for living out of a rhythm of both solitude and community. Taking time away was significant for him, perhaps undergirding the times of extending transformative love and presence that we witness in the Gospel stories.

I invite you to ponder: What fills my being with truth? What restores my mind and heart?

What helps me thrive on a weekly/monthly/quarterly/annual basis? What do I need to place in my schedule to help honour my life? Ponder! Dream with Divine Love! Love your life! Spend time with your wonderful self! Your life of service will be the *overflow* of this rich gift of time you have given yourself.

Chapter III

You Don't Know Anything and You Have Everything You Need

One of the most significant gifts we tap into as we offer Spiritual Direction is our ability to listen to our intuition. As we listen to others, we need to, as Joy explained, listen to the words that are being said and those that are not being said. This takes profound attentiveness and awareness. There is a balance we're invited to hold as we use our intuition in service to other people's lives.

I read a novel about Spiritual Direction[5] that I have pondered a great deal. The main character had a superb gift of intuition. He could *read* people easily, and as he learned this about himself, it gave him a sense of great confidence in the gift. Eventually it made him overconfident, and he overstepped a boundary when he assumed something to be true that was not. His mentor admonished him to always remember that he *could* be wrong. You don't *know* anything for sure. We may intuit a great deal, but we need to hold this knowing with an inner posture of *not-knowing*.

Many people in some sort of spiritual caregiving role are very intuitive. Once someone turned to me at a retreat and said, "I know that you *know*." At that moment, I think he intuited a knowing in me more than I knew of myself. Over the years, I've come to be in relationship with this inner *knowing*. We *know* things! As I listen to others, my

....

5   Susan Howatch, Mystical Paths (New York: Ballantine Books, 1992), 396

intuition kicks in, and I sense all sorts of things. I intuit moods, experiences, and feelings in others to whom I am present. I am aware of a lot; however, I also have an inner smile as I hear myself being reminded in the midst of my intuition: "You don't *know* anything." I don't take this as derogatory or a put down but as a mentor speaking firmly to me: "Remember to walk with wonder, curiosity, humility, and tenderness!"

> *"Remember to walk with wonder,*
> *curiosity, humility, and tenderness!"*

Guest at the Table

In Spiritual Direction, I am listening to another life. I really don't know anything ... even when I think I do! That person has a unique story, and I am a witness to that story. It's so easy to project my story or the hundreds of other stories I've heard onto this new story. But the truth is, I don't *know* anything. This is where I need to position myself—as a *guest* at the table of another person's life. They are inviting me to sit with them, and I'm there to learn, listen, ask questions, observe, notice, and mostly, love.

Many times I've listened to others and realized that elements of their story were similar to mine. A part of me wanted to say, "I totally understand." But the truth is, I don't. Even if our situations are similar, they've had a completely different life experience. My job is to witness with full attention their experience, their story.

Intuition as Service

One of our greatest gifts as Spiritual Directors is our intuition. This gift is meant to *serve* the ones we listen to and to lead us toward asking questions and discovery. A practical way to use our intuition is to say something like: "I have a sense about this situation. Does the following thought resonate with you in any way?" This way, our directees can be the ones to determine what is true for themselves.

Trusting Our Intuition

For some of us, learning to trust our deep instincts, inner knowing, and intuition hasn't been easy. Coming out of a fundamentalist Christian background, I was taught to distrust my knowing and to be suspicious of the intuition I carry. I was taught that the deepest part of me was corrupt. How could I ever trust it? Part of my healing has been to understand that this knowing and awareness that lives within me is a beautiful gift to be *cherished and nurtured*. Awareness of Original Blessing, as opposed to Original Sin, shifted my understanding to open to the goodness within. As J. Philip Newell says: "Conscience, and the inner capacity to know what is right and what is wrong, are rooted in the original righteousness of the soul, and the goodness of the image in which we are made has not been lost."[6]

Trusting that intuition may point the way, while listening to someone in Spiritual Direction has been key to unlocking truth in many sessions. As I have learned to trust this inner gift, I hold it with humility and wonder when I stand before another life.

Intuition Is a Grace

The stronger the intuition, the more I need to remember this. As I work with the inner awareness that comes in a session with an individual, directees are often deeply moved at the accuracy of a question or a pondering I may express. Their gratitude and wonder may fuel my sense of accomplishment and pride in what has transpired. I may be tempted to identify the gift of intuition with my persona.

Once again, I hear these words with a chuckle: "Cathy, you don't know anything." If I've been able to accompany someone and be helpful, *it is a grace we have both received*. I am also invited to wonder with awe that the Infinite is moving to illuminate and bring truth to

6   J. Philip Newell, Listening for the Heartbeat of God (London: Paulist Press, 1997), 16

another. The awareness that this experience is a *grace* continues to give me peace. It fuels my desire to be attentive and to continue to listen to the One who loves the other more.

Everything I Need
In this way, I have everything I need! Partnership with Wisdom holds all I need as I am present to another. My work is to become attentive to how Love might be loving that individual. If I align myself with Love, then Love will guide the intuition I receive, our conversation, and the awareness of the individual to receive what they need.

Chapter IV

Expect to Be Triggered and See It as a Gift

One of the things that happened to me when I was a child was a situation of emotional exploitation. A family member who was under duress began to confide in me when I was very young. They didn't mean to hurt me intentionally, but it harmed me greatly. I began to carry emotional responsibility for someone far older than myself and to feel the weight of their wellbeing on my shoulders for years to come. It wasn't until my mid-thirties that I began to identify how much this had impacted me, and how the patterns learned in this relationship impacted so many other relationships in my adult life.

Hooks from the Past

I began to understand that from the time I was very young, I naturally listened to others and became the caregiver. When others had emotional expectations, I saw it as my duty and responsibility to fulfill them. I didn't set personal boundaries around my own emotional health, allowing people to take advantage of my heart. It was a very hard learning experience for me when I realized that I didn't have to do that anymore. Over the next fifteen years, establishing emotional boundaries was a muscle I worked hard on developing.

When I became a Spiritual Director in my early fifties, I recognized a few situations in which I was being triggered. I could feel the emotional expectation to give more than was appropriate for the relationship. I could feel the yearning, the longing, the need! My heart would race, and I would struggle in myself, as I would sometimes over-give once again. I would recognize after a session that I had been caught in an old pattern. I was being called to face it and strengthen that muscle even more.

It created tension in me to turn toward what drove me to that behaviour in the first place. I had to face my fears of rejection and not being "enough" for another. I had to kneel down and pray for help to know what was mine to do and what was not. These moments were difficult for me but they were also like a flashlight shining on the shadows of my life; revealing the places in me that needed strengthening.

Hooks in Spiritual Direction
Other times as people shared their stories, I'd remember stories of my own. Some of my own trauma would rise in my body, and the longing to project my own experience, anger, frustration, and judgement would be right there. I was triggered by what I was hearing. Body sensations are a significant aspect of being triggered, as the blood rushes, the heart races, and the mind becomes frantic. This body awareness serves as a red flag. Notice! Notice! Notice!

At these moments, an icon in the room, such as a stone or another symbol of Love's presence, can help to ground us in the present moment. When we're triggered, we're carried to the past and are no longer fully present to the moment before us. Returning to our breath, returning to Love's Presence, returning to the person in front of us is where we are invited to be.

Allowing ourselves to settle again may take time. In moments like these, I invite the directee and myself into times of silence. I allow myself to reorient. I return to the present. I then listen. Listen! Listen to guidance for the next step.

Sometimes an image will come, or perhaps a question or insight. As I allow my personal reaction to step off of the stage, Love's guidance has room to take centre stage, and we can move forward. Awareness is the key to our listening: What is happening for me? How am I respond-ing/reacting? What is happening for the other? How can I serve?

Awareness is the key to our listening:
What is happening for me?
How am I responding/reacting?
What is happening for the other?
How can I serve?

Silence and Stillness Lead to Wisdom

Sometimes, I have to really wait before that direction is clear. To rest in silence with another can be difficult, but it's a place of humility and trust. Sometimes the directee will be the one to break the silence because the silence has given room for them to have an awareness or an epiphany. Sometimes when things are still unknown for me, I'll ask the question: "What are you becoming aware of in the silence?"

This is constantly the invitation for ourselves and those we are directing. We are invited to become *aware*, to *wake up* in the midst of whatever we're going through to the movement of Love in our lives. As directors, we need to always be open to this awareness, and we teach others that they can become aware too. Awareness opens the door to wisdom and leads us toward the process of transformation.

Chapter V

Surprised by Gifts of Grace

One day I entered a Spiritual Direction session feeling more depleted than I wanted to be. Some things in my personal life had happened the day before that had distracted my heart and caused some anxiety. I knew I wasn't as centred and grounded as I like to feel before a session, so I asked the Presence of Love for grace for the session with this person and that I would still be able to be present to her life and what she was bringing that day.

As she began to share, I was surprised at the inner struggle she was telling me about. It resonated with my own story from the day before. And then with firmness and conviction, she quoted a passage of scripture that had come to her in the midst of her distress.

I knew in that moment that I was being present to this person's life, but that Mystery was also being present to me. Those words were like an arrow in my heart, reminding me of the Living Presence's profound presence in the midst of my own story as I listened to another soul. Tears came close to me as I sensed the Eternal's care in the room—care for the one telling her story, and care for my own heart.

This kind of situation has happened more than once, and I'm amazed and also filled with humility at how Love reminds me that we're all "walking each other home." These moments are unexpected gifts of grace. As we're attentive to others, we may encounter a surprise coming toward us at the same time. As much as we're able in these moments, we need to receive the gift and then set it aside for later personal reflection, bringing our attentiveness again fully to the one before us. But as we do so, our hearts can swell and sing out "*Thank you.*"

Chapter VI

Presence Is Enough

*"Our most important question as healers is not, 'What to say or to do?'
but, 'How to develop enough inner space where the story can be received?'
Healing is the humble but also very demanding task of creating and
offering a friendly empty space where strangers can reflect on their pain
and suffering without fear, and find the confidence that makes them look
for new ways right in the center of their confusion."*

Henri J.M. Nouwen[7]

I believe there is a profound human need that each of us carries to be witnessed, to be seen, to be heard, to be known. This is the gift we offer to others through Spiritual Direction. It's a gift with the potential to create space for profound healing and transformation. As Spiritual Directors, we can become enamored with creating the hopeful end result and lose sight of the simplicity of our role—to offer presence.

....

7   Henri J. M. Nouwen, Reaching Out (New York: Doubleday, 1975), 97

What Is Our Motivation?

Many of us enter the calling of Spiritual Direction truly wanting to offer this gift of presence to others, but we must examine our underlying motivation as we move into service for others. There's a difference between the posture of service and the posture of helping. We must examine this desire to help. Why do we want to help? What motivates our vocational path? What draws us to sit with others and hear their stories?

Why do we want to help?
What motivates our vocational path?
What draws us to sit with others and hear their stories?

Are we "helping" to meet a need in ourselves?
Are we "helping" to heal a wound in our lives?
Are we "helping" to distract us from our own inner work?

Are we "helping" to meet a need in ourselves? Are we "helping" to heal a wound in our lives? Are we "helping" to distract us from our own inner work? When we move into a vocation of service from subconscious motivations that are about our own need to help, we can become very *attached to outcome*. When I am attached to outcome, I can *no longer be present*. Suddenly, instead of being present, my worth, value, and significance is tied up in *if I am successful* in helping the other. My needs are met by the other's progress toward wholeness. I become outcome-oriented instead of present in the moment. My desire lies in finding solutions and fixing problems rather than sitting with possible tension or discomfort. However, *it is in the very tension and discomfort* that we need to be present.

Called to Presence

People are looking for problem solvers! However, the role of the Spiritual Director is not to problem solve but to be *present with the problem*. This means sitting with tension and discomfort with *possibly no answers*. This means untangling ourselves from the role of hero and saviour and simply being present with the difficulty and the not-knowing. We are invited to trust that a deep wisdom lies within the directee that they can learn to access. This releases us from over-functioning and instead allows us to be in the here and now, offering a spacious presence.

Questions for Listening in the Tension

+ *What anxiety/fear is arising with the current circumstance the directee is labelling a problem?*
+ *How does this current anxiety/fear invite the directee to deeper trust?*
+ *How is this current problem an archetype of a larger pattern in the directee's life that she/he is being called to face?*
+ *What is the invitation that the Divine is whispering in the midst of this problem?*
+ *What is the directee learning through being in this problem now that is grace?*
+ *What is the directee being invited to let go of?*
+ *What is he/she being invited to receive?*
+ *What might be a hidden journey of lament that is necessary at this time?*
+ *Where are the hidden tears being locked up? Why?*
+ *What are the temptations that are leading the directee away from being present to their suffering?*
+ *How can the directee be aware of Love's presence now, in the midst of suffering?*
+ *What do we become aware of when we enter silence in our suffering?*

Allowing ourselves to *be in the tension* of life with others allows people to stay in their own story and do their own inner work. We can't help people do their work, but we can be present, offer questions, and give tools to help them listen to their precious souls. Allowing times of silence in these moments of acknowledging the pain, suffering, and challenge can be a great tool for guiding someone to *be with* themselves in ways that perhaps haven't felt safe before. We are a culture of running away from anything awkward. Being with our pain is terribly awkward. We might feel angry! We might cry! We might be very uncomfortable.

Tension of Feelings

As Spiritual Directors, it's very important to allow uncomfortable moments into our sacred space. Allowing discomfort invites us to go deeper. What is underneath the discomfort? When we are able to remain calm in the midst of intense emotion, a zone of safety is created where feelings can be explored, perhaps for the first time. Most of us have forgotten even how to feel; we *think* our feelings instead of allowing our bodies to inhabit the feeling. We have censored feelings as good or bad instead of noticing, allowing, and turning toward all of them. Suppressed feelings are like balls in water. They may be pushed down for a time, but they will always pop up somewhere else.

Feelings are an essential element of our truth-telling. When a soul can acknowledge awkward and hard feelings, it leads to deeper and deeper truths that are yearning to be heard, felt, and expressed. We can perhaps learn to know ourselves for the first time when we engage honestly with our feelings. Being able to *feel* our pain and *express* the deep truth within us without shame or judgement is healing and restorative, opening the door for soul friendship with ourselves.

Present to Ourselves as We Are Present to Others

As Spiritual Directors, we're invited to notice and become aware of what is arising in us so that we can do our own inner work. This allows us to be a clear mirror for those we're listening to. When people come with their problems, fears, and anxieties it can evoke our own struggles. Instead of responding with presence, we respond with fixing. Why? Does it calm our own fears? Does it soothe our own anxiety? What are we afraid of if we can't fix the difficulty? What is showing up for us? Why can't we sit with another's discomfort?

As spiritual companions, we're invited to be unattached to outcome and progress (as we would define it or measure it). We are invited to simply BE with another ... with our full presence. This full presence holds the space for profound trust, *a trust in the other* and that the answers to their problem *lie within them* and their connection with inner wisdom. It's a trust that Love is holding and loving them far more than we can with our human understanding.

Spaciousness in Formation

Sometimes the very act of *understanding the problem* is the opposite of what the Spirit is inviting us to. Part of spiritual formation is to enter the *unknown,* to yield to a mystery, to hidden places, to obscurity, both in ourselves and in those we're listening to. We are not to rush understanding. We are not to rush healing. We are not to rush formation.

We are not to rush understanding.
We are not to rush healing.
We are not to rush formation.

This soul journey is a mystery that is not our *doing* but rather our simple participation of holy presence. There's a quality of spaciousness here that may seem empty or useless. Not rescuing or having answers, sitting in silence, and allowing space may seem without value, but these are the qualities where a soul can be re-born. If we are anxious to fill the empty spaces, we may abort the work that is slow and full of mystery. Spaciousness, if we can step back and allow it, is full of the holy. Awareness arises from the roots of stillness and silence. Wisdom arises from surrender to darkness and formation. Compassion arises from grace received in times of brokenness. Transformation arises from knowing unconditional love.

There are so many measuring tools that we constantly use to validate our work and measure our success. However, the art of Spiritual Direction is not about measuring. It is about a profound stillness of being where we witness another soul without judgement, allowing that soul to be met in love and grace and mercy. When we are able to hold that space with love and grace, we will stand on the precipice of the miracle of a soul coming home.

Awareness arises
From the roots of stillness and silence.
Wisdom arises
From surrender to darkness and formation.
Compassion arises
From grace received in times of brokenness.
Transformation arises
From knowing unconditional love.

Chapter VII

Setting the Table

Setting the table is an act of love that we do as we prepare to eat a meal with others. When I walk into a home that has been lovingly prepared for a shared meal, I feel so grateful—there is a sense of being cared for, thought of, loved! "Setting the table" in Spiritual Direction is so significant; it's about preparing a beautiful space for a soul through our presence, the space, our words, and silence. Setting the table for a directee sends a profound message to the one coming that they truly matter and their lives are important. Perhaps they don't treat their lives as important, but we can show through how we prepare for them that their lives truly matter and that they're worth setting a table for.

Preparing My Own Heart

To sit with another person is sacred, so to rush into an appointment doesn't allow for my own heart to settle and be fully present. This time of listening in Spiritual Direction is one-sided. I need to leave my own story at the door to be prepared to fully engage with the person I'm listening to. I may have just had a difficult phone call with a family member, found out that an appliance is broken and I'm facing a huge bill, or been struggling with a difficult decision (all of which have happened to me). But as I walk into that Spiritual Direction room, it's time for me to entrust my life into Love's hands for this time, leaving it at the door.

Taking a few minutes before a directee comes helps me to let go of what's happening in my own story. I must focus my attention on their lives, their story, their journey. I take time to listen to a poem or writing that can be a meditation tool for us to begin with. I light the candle. Sometimes I just sit in silence. The important thing is to take some time for this transition—the transition of being fully present to another.

One person told me that she sat in her car before the appointment just knowing I was sitting inside waiting for her. Somehow, knowing I was waiting for her, being in silence on her behalf, gave her comfort and a sense of being loved and valued. But it is for both of us that this time is important. I need to let go of what's occupying my mind and turn my gaze toward her life. By the time the directee walks in, the table is set and ready for them.

Words of Meditation, Silence, and Invitation

I have found that the first few moments of a session are significant for laying the foundation and setting the tone of the time together. These moments are like the opening course of a meal. Many people aren't sure what they want to share about in their times of Spiritual Direction. Taking the first five to ten minutes to become still and listen can help the directee notice what is arising in them that perhaps they didn't know before. Written meditations, poetry, and prayer exercises are found in many resources offering possible words to begin a session. Some of my favourite books to draw from are: *Celtic Benediction*,[8] *Psalms for Praying*,[9] and *Prayer Seeds*.[10]

Taking time to listen to a reading helps focus both the director and the directee on being attentive to presence. Instead of a reading, a song

---

8   J. Philip Newell, Celtic Benediction (Toronto: Novalis, 2001).

9   Nan C. Merrill, Psalms for Praying (London: Bloomsbury, 2007).

10   Joyce Rupp, Prayer Seeds (Notre Dame: Sorin Books, 2017).

of meditation from a recording can also be a great gift to both director and directee for slowing down and listening to their own soul. Another form of meditation to use at the beginning of a session could be an image or icon that the directee may want to hold or look at. Sometimes an image will grab someone's attention as they enter a space. I have learned to notice those moments and invite directees to sit with that image as we begin our time together.

Using some form of meditation to begin a session reminds both the director and directee that they are both listening to the sacredness of a life and are not simply focused on each other. This is a time to be aware of what is both transcendent and grounding. There may be other forms of creating stillness and awareness that you develop. The important thing is that your heart is ready to fully welcome the other so they have a space where they can slow down, breathe, and become attentive to their own heart.

Samples of a Beginning of a Session:

Sample 1

Director: *Peter, I'm so glad to see you.*
Peter: It's good to be back!
Director: *How was your Christmas break?*
Peter: Overall, it was pretty good, although I found it really stressful when Sally got sick.
             We had to go to the hospital for a few days.
Director: *I was sad to hear about that, Peter. You and Sally have been on my mind.*
             I was grateful to know she's okay. If you would like to explore how Sally's hospitalization impacted you, please feel free to bring that forward in our time together.
             Why don't we begin our time with a reading and silence?
Peter: Yes, that would be good.

Director:	*Let's begin by slowing down and being aware of our breath as prayer. (Take a moment to just be still and breathe together.)*
	Here's a reading from this book of prayers. (Read slowly and let the words sink into your own heart as you become even more present to Peter, to Love.)
	Let's pause now and be silent for a moment together. (Take a moment for silence.)
	We dedicate this sacred time to listening, being attentive, and listening to your soul. We trust that Love is holding and sustaining us both as we enter this hour. (Take a transition moment in which you can offer an intention or a prayer that can guide the directee toward the next step.)
	Peter, you can stay in silence as long as you need to, but when you're ready to share, I'm here for you.
Peter:	I didn't know what I was going to talk about, but in the silence, I remembered a dream from last night. Could we begin there?

Sample 2

Sally:	Whoa! Am I ever glad to be here. I am so stressed out (tears erupt).
Director:	*I am here for you Sally. Please come in and get comfortable.*
Sally:	Okay, so remember about my mom and all that was

	going on last month? (Sally begins to talk immediately and goes into great detail about issues that have been painful for her with her mom.)
Director:	*Sally, perhaps we can just pause a moment. Why don't we ground ourselves together in some silence and beauty? Would you be open to that?*
Sally:	Oh, okay. Yeah. That might be good for me to slow down and catch my breath.
Director:	*Why don't we say this breath prayer silently together:*

I come ... as I am.

I come ... as I am.

(allowing some space)

Let's just breathe in silence together and become aware of Presence.

(Use this time of silence to hold Sally in love and pray for wisdom for the session and an awareness of wisdom underneath the emotional chaos that Sally has entered in with.)

Let's listen to this meditative chant and allow it to be our prayer. (Listen together to the recording.)

Whatever needs to be heard, whatever needs to be held, whatever needs to be seen, we invite that into this sacred space of grace and mercy.

Sally, whenever you're ready, I'm here for you.

Sally: Thank you. In the silence, I became aware of my anxiety and fear. I also became aware of Love with me in the midst of this. Perhaps it would be helpful to unpack what created this anxiety today. Perhaps I need more help with my rhythms of prayer so I can live out of greater awareness. Could we talk about those things?

At the time of this writing, I connected with someone who had come for Spiritual Direction a few years prior. She wrote to me about her memories:

"One cold winter afternoon, I walked into Cathy's sacred space. She had the candles lit by the 'circle of friendship.' I was greeted with her smile and compassionate eyes ... a warm blanket, and of course her hug ... which heals. This thought flashed through my mind: 'Warmed by the fire of the Holy Spirit's friendship.'"

Chapter VIII

Trauma: Yours and Theirs

I hesitate to talk about trauma as I'm not an expert in the subject. However, I find the courage to say a few things around this important aspect of Spiritual Direction when I share simply from my own personal experience of how these two things are connected.

Responding as Spiritual Caregivers

I have realized that many spiritual leaders/facilitators are uncomfortable and feel ill-equipped when a person with post trauma is triggered. When trauma is triggered, sometimes the individual displays an intense physical and/or emotional reaction. How we respond to trauma can either intensify the person's pain or create a healing space for the person to be with their pain. Spiritual Directors are not therapists, so our job is not to explore the trauma in the same way a therapist would. However, we can offer a loving and gentle presence that can be profoundly healing in and of itself. I believe it's imperative that we, as spiritual companions, become informed about trauma so that we're aware of symptoms and dynamics that may arise as we sit with those in need.

Experiences—Being Held

I've experienced something called chronic post traumatic syndrome in my own life. It's experienced when one is living with a long-term stressful situation and has a feeling of being on high alert for an extended period of years. When I was no longer in that situation, I could be triggered to feel the same things I did when I was in the stressful atmosphere. I never knew what would trigger me, but when it would come (through a situation or conversation that evoked the memories of what I had lived with), my heart would start racing and I'd have trouble breathing. My whole body felt impacted, and I'd need to go to a quiet place and reassure myself that I was all right. Slowly, my breathing would return to normal and my heart would settle. One time when I was unexpectedly triggered, I just happened to be sitting by a loving friend. She recognized what was happening and didn't become flustered. She simply put her arm around me and breathed with me until I settled. Her calm energy and presence brought my anxious heart a message that I was okay and would be okay. This experience was incredibly healing and filled with grace. There was no shame or judgement in her quiet presence, just love.

Experience—Being Shamed

Another time when I was triggered, I was a student in a group experience. I recognized that those in charge of the meeting didn't know what to do as I struggled to breathe and the bodily symptoms of trauma manifested themselves so I left the room to care for myself. Later, one of the facilitators came to me and said these words: "I'm sure glad you know how to take care of that beast." Those words were very painful to me at the time. I felt shamed about what had happened instead of knowing compassion. That experience motivated me to develop a greater consciousness toward others who might have post-trauma stress and to hold kindness and compassion for their story as much as I could.

Trauma in Spiritual Direction

A few years later as I began a full-time Spiritual Direction practice and individuals began to share their stories, some of them experienced post-traumatic body sensations during the sessions because they were opening up their lives in new ways. Memories were being opened that were connected to their current spiritual growth. Facing what happened in the past was a necessity in opening up to Divine Love in greater measure; however, turning toward the past brought panic and post-trauma sensations. In those moments, I sought to create a calm and loving atmosphere, assuring the person that I was with them and breathing with them until they felt settled again. At times, I sought permission to sit beside them until they were ready to sit alone again. Being with pain is tough, but it doesn't last forever. *No matter how deep the trauma, Love is deeper.* This is what I hold in my heart in these moments.

No matter
how deep the trauma,
Love is deeper.

Other Support for Trauma

I also recognize that these moments can reveal the necessity of having another professional involved in the directee's life who can explore with care the origins of the trauma and provide therapeutic help. Those who have experienced sexual assault, abuse, or abandonment can be greatly helped by seeing a therapist in addition to a Spiritual Director to assist in working with the trauma from different angles. It's so helpful if we know some therapists we can trust and have as references to send people to for the areas that need extra care. Suggesting the need for extra therapeutic help is always done sensitively after the intense physical and emotional process has settled.

I do feel that we can offer the gift of healing presence as trauma emerges unexpectedly in the room, even as we send directees for additional support elsewhere. If we can learn about trauma, how it manifests, and what's happening to the person on a physiological level, then we won't be shaken or surprised when it arises. We can be a container of love and grace.

Trauma in Ourselves

As stated in an earlier chapter, we may continue to carry our own trauma and be surprised by being triggered as we listen to other people's stories. We can't stop a session and focus on ourselves, but we can invite the session to pause and take the opportunity to find our ground again, noting that we have work to do with ourselves later on. It's always humbling to recognize our unfinished work, but we're all an unfinished symphony. None of our songs are yet complete. Our imperfection is like the diminished chord in music. It's the chord that holds an element of tension in it that leads to the chord of the tonic, the place where the song feels and sounds like "home." The beauty of our lives is the melody that's being played, and we're not yet finished composing this song. There is no shame in acknowledging our need to process another element of our journey, another phrase in our composition. The more we continue to do our own work in noticing what is happening for us, the more present we can continue to be for those we serve.

Breathing With

As people walk in the door, we never really know what will happen. Trauma is one of the guests that may arrive. I invite us into the posture of *breathing with* those in pain and trusting that Love in the room will guide the moments until the heart again can come to rest. In this way, we can identify with what Dr. Edith Eva Eger, Auschwitz survivor and clinical therapist writes: "To heal we embrace the dark. We walk through the shadow of the valley on our way to the light."[11]

---

11   Dr. Edith Eva Eger, The Choice (New York: Scribner, 2017), 224.

Chapter IX

Perspectives from the Piano Bench

Lessons from the Piano Bench

As I began working more in accompanying others in soul work, I began to see the relevance of all that I had learned as a piano teacher with Spiritual Direction. For thirty-six years I sat one-on-one with individuals at the piano bench, from four-year-olds to seventy-year-olds. When I began, I struggled to be an effective teacher. I realized I didn't know how to teach. My students were failing at learning and weren't retaining information. They didn't really understand how to read the music and didn't seem motivated to practise. I became motivated to *learn* how to teach, how to communicate. I became curious, especially about children, who made up the majority of my students. How does a child learn? How does a child become motivated? How does a child take in new information? All this learning over the next three decades brought me surprised understanding in the Spiritual Direction room many years later.

Each Individual Is Unique

As I taught, I began to realize that each child that came in the door was unique. What would work for teaching one child wouldn't work with teaching the next. I had to learn to be *attentive to each person* and learn what would "catch" their interest, their style of learning. I always had to meet them where they were at, and that meant I had to understand their frame of reference to a certain extent. I realized that some students grasped linear learning easily. It seemed like breathing to them. But they didn't know how to *feel* the music. Other students were so intuitive they could grasp the emotional content of a song long before they understood how to actually read the music. Some students couldn't learn at all because they were blocked by emotional matters at home or at school. I remember one student who just lay on the floor with my dog for five minutes at the beginning of the lesson to receive some level of comfort before she could focus on learning.

In the same way, as people began to come for Spiritual Direction, I needed to see each one as unique—coming with their own unique needs, desires, and pain. Instead of being filled with answers, I reminded myself to be filled with curiosity. *What story did they bring? What made them come to life? What depleted them? What did they long for? What did they grieve? What blocked them from receiving?* As I held back assumptions about each individual and approached them as beings that I could also learn and grow from, there was grace to respond to each person in a unique way. Spiritual Direction then became highly individualized, an art form to live into with each person.

Practising Together

I also learned that I could tell music students to go and practise, but unless they were motivated and guided well, 90 per cent of them would struggle with a daily routine of sitting at the piano. I found that if I sat on the piano bench with a student during the lesson and we *played the music together*, the confidence would begin to grow that they could actually play the piece by themselves at home. Playing the piano can be a solitary experience, so fostering a sense of doing it together when they were with me helped to encourage the student to continue playing at home.

In the same way, in Spiritual Direction I realized that we needed to *practise together* modes of contemplation, stillness, being with our pain, receiving grace, etc. We needed to make these abstract concepts a reality to really know. And we needed to do that together. I learned to incorporate into the Spiritual Direction sessions moments of practising together these various spiritual exercises so that the directee could feel accompanied in learning these forms and possibly make them a life-long discipline and pathway of transformation.

Beauty of the Pause
A key element in music is the pause, the space in between. Teaching children that the rest in a musical score had as much value as the note expressed became a beautiful metaphor for Spiritual Direction. The sounds of music are poignant because of the spaces. If we don't allow space in music, we experience cacophony. Why do we resist the spaces of our lives?

Creating a joyful sense of anticipation in the spaces of music helped to bring fun, joy, and celebration into what was coming next as I sat with a child at the piano. In life, the spaces are often times when we don't know what's coming, so we resist the unknown, the pause. Spiritual Direction offers a place where we can remember that the pauses of our lives are just as significant as action. The music of our life is birthed in both the spaces of emptiness and the expression of fullness.

> *The music of our life is birthed*
> *in both the spaces of emptiness*
> *and the expression of fullness.*

Carrying Our Inner Child
Another element I became familiar with was the energy of different age groups. Five-year-olds are not all the same, of course, but there can be some interesting similarities. Twelve-year-old girls carry some shared qualities, and fifteen-year old boys have some ways of being in common. Four-year-olds, eight-year olds ... each age became a fascination for me, something to learn about. After so many years of sitting

for hours with each age, I learned. I learned and learned and learned. In Spiritual Direction, I began to notice that sometimes people would be responding to a difficult or painful situation in their life with physical manifestations. Tones of voice and body expressions reminded me of the different ages of my music students. A fifty-year-old woman would suddenly remind me of a six-year-old. A seventy-year-old man would suddenly make me remember a fifteen-year-old student. I became curious about the "ages of us." We all carry inside the ages we've been. Sometimes we get stuck at an age due to a trauma. Something later in life can trigger that place in us, creating a powerful opportunity to revisit and heal the past wound.

These moments, although sometimes needing referral to therapists, can be moments of pause and reflection. Questions can be asked in Spiritual Direction that might allow the directee to experience greater self-awareness and perhaps the desire to face some unfinished inner work.

I notice there's a certain energy when you revisit that memory. What's happening for you internally?
Do you feel a certain age inside of you as you say those words?
If we slow down and breathe together, what do you notice?
Are you able to hold compassion towards your younger self?
If you imagine Love/Christ sitting beside you now, what do you become aware of?

By paying attention to moments like this, which are usually unconscious, we can create a possibility of allowing the person to deepen in awareness of themselves, healing of the past, and greater consciousness.

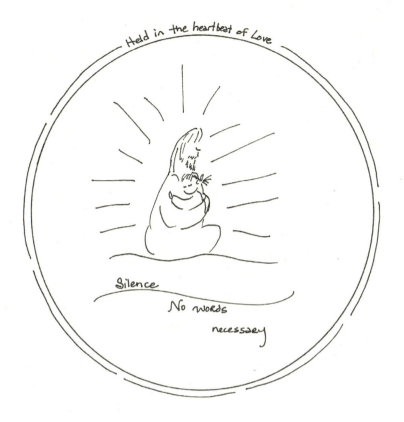

Held in the heartbeat of Love

Silence

No words

necessary

Judith

Allowing the inner child to emerge in a session is a vulnerable act for the directee; it's an act of trust as the child reveals its truth. Judith had been doing a lot of her own inner work with a therapist but came on a Soul Care Retreat and asked for a session together. As we sat down, she shared with me about the journey she'd been on with listening to her inner child, recognizing that her inner child was taking responsibility for everything and was oh-so-tired. She was learning to notice her inner child's longings for play and rest. In our conversation, she related how the retreat was impacting her. A traumatic memory emerged that blocked her from trusting in the Divine.

Why did that terrible thing happen?
How could "God" have allowed that?

These questions emerged from a very tender place. Important questions. Serious questions. But instead of pausing with these questions, Judith began speaking quickly about all the ways she was coping with these questions, giving various reasonable explanations. I invited her to return to the questions of her inner child. What did her inner child really need with these questions?

Judith turned to me with sudden awareness. This inner child needed *validation*, not answers. These were important questions that needed kindness, empathy, and attention. No logical answer would bring the satisfaction that the inner child longed for. Judith turned toward her own dear heart and just allowed the questions to be. This began a beautiful process in her for the rest of the retreat, a process of her turning toward her inner child with kindness, attentiveness, and *without answers*. In a surprising way, the rest of the retreat brought more closure to Judith on this issue. It became a time full of healing and grace.

Need for Validation

Children need to be seen, recognized, validated. Sitting with a student on the piano bench was a time of saying *I see you; you are important to me, and your experience is valid*. When children felt seen and validated in the music studio, they flourished because they felt believed in. They worked hard and they rose to heights they didn't even know possible. That child within us is often still looking for a place of validation and of being witnessed. Spiritual Direction can be a place where the inner child can know the gift of being recognized and cherished.

Different Lengths of Time

Many music students stayed with me over long periods of time. One student stayed with me from the time she was four until she was twenty. We had a long relationship through music lessons and are still connected today. Other students came for a few sessions but then realized it wasn't their thing. Spiritual Direction can be like that too. We journey with people for various lengths of time. It's their choice of how long they decide to walk with us, so we must count it all as a gift. We must also realize that one session may stay with a person for life. Things I have spoken in Spiritual Direction were remembered and held in the heart by someone who recently found me again after ten years. Each session must be held as sacred, a grace of one soul witnessing another.

Chapter X

Stay Close to Yourself

Doreen, the Spiritual Director I've journeyed with for the past many years, has been a treasure chest of musings, thoughts, and sayings. Often, as I would walk out her door, she would look me in the eye and say, "Go gently, Cathy." Sayings like this would make me ponder during the hour drive home. What does it mean to "go gently?" These were words I didn't usually hear when saying goodbye to another. But with Doreen, every word said out loud was thought through, intentional, breathed with prayer, lived before spoken, and saturated in silence. And so, I would ponder and ponder. Then I would let go of trying to *get it* ... because these little sayings always felt just beyond my grasp. However, there would come a day, often a year or two later, when the phrase would drop into my heart. Perhaps it would be like a seed that's finally germinating in the soil of my being. Then I could *feel* it and *know* it for the first time.

Going Gently—An Inner Posture

"Going gently," I began to understand over a long period of pondering, was an inner posture of the heart, a *way* of being, the ground of transformation. Everything around me in the culture was screaming to go faster, achieve more, be successful (whatever that means), push through, etc. Going gently was to foster a different rhythm than the one pounding in my ears. Going gently was to become attuned with my soul and aware of the subtle gifts, the quiet gifts, the gentle gifts that were always waiting there for me if I paid attention. In this way, I also learned that Spiritual Direction was a long-term companionship in *walking the way*. It was different than my therapeutic experiences, one with a psychologist and the other with a Jungian analyst, both of which were profound gifts in my life. I was becoming aware that the intention of Spiritual Direction was to learn a new way of walking, a walk that may take years, perhaps a lifetime. The journey of Spiritual Direction was a soul invitation, an invitation to reorient my whole life to walk a way that was congruent with my true self.

The Walk of Spiritual Direction

This way of the soul signaled a quiet walk, a gentle way, a *hidden* journey. Spiritual Direction, in my mind, has often been like entering the woods, going to a hidden hut, and sitting with a wise soul. This soul knows the way of the woods, the pathways of the heart that are not always clear to the masses. This way isn't filled with titles or acknowledgement, praise or glory. It is obscure. It is dark at times. It is fraught with tangled branches and overgrown pathways. But if one keeps returning, year after year, the pathways open and a walk, a beautiful walk, emerges. One realizes over time that many precious souls have also come here. But one must have the courage to enter the woods alone.

Go gently.

As I have journeyed with Doreen over the years, she has been that wise soul in the depths of the forest, teaching me of the way of the heart. She heard me express my frustrations, my longings, my fears, my hopes, and my places of confusion. I would be consumed with the "situation" or the "person" who was making my life difficult (or so I thought). I would be gripped by fear and struggling with making decisions. Over and over and over again, Doreen would direct me back to my inner life, my heart, and the places where I was being hooked out of my own story.

Stay Close to Yourself

Reaching into her treasure chest, another phrase was brought to my attention: "Cathy, stay close to yourself." Perhaps this phrase could be understood as an invitation to be self-consumed or self-centred. Rather, it was the invitation to look at the shadows *in myself* rather than the shadows in another. It required, over and over again, a willingness to face my own heart instead of blaming another or a circumstance for my unhappiness. Staying close to myself meant turning toward my fears and insecurities. Staying close to myself was difficult. It was much easier to be a victim, to blame, to speculate on how things could be better.

Staying close to myself meant cleaning out my own inner closets and eventually becoming a deep friend to my own heart. I was invited to turn toward the parts of myself that had been shamed, distanced, ostracized, betrayed, abused, etc. I was invited to hold and care for all of me, and thus open the door for an integration of being rooted and grounded in Love. As this work of staying close to myself deepened over many years, the compulsion to blame or get caught up in the drama of a circumstance lessened. I found my inner roots deepening and an ability to draw from the inner wellsprings become a place of rest and stability. What a long journey this has been and continues to be.

Stay close to yourself.

Of course, I still get hooked by people and circumstances and still can get caught up in the drama of life. But this journey of staying close to myself has been like an inner forest crew of trailblazers, building and clearing new paths within. These inner roads to my soul were wild and filled with debris at the beginning. I would bump along with many crashes along the way. But over time, these roads have become smoother, and the sign-posts have become old friends.

Inviting Others to Stay Close to Themselves— The Journey in and Down

As I now listen to other people's stories, I recognize the tendency in others to become fixated on a situation or a person they are describing. This is all they can see. It's like they're riding the waves of their life and it's a wild and stormy sea. I can sense that they'd like me to help them calm the sea down, or come with a helicopter and take them out of the churning waters. Doreen's words come to me in these moments: *stay close to yourself.* I wonder how we can shift the focus from the outer waves to what lies underneath all the drama? I wonder if we can shift from the raging energy to a quiet and still place that is within each one of us, the place close to our souls? Our souls carry the stillness *underneath* the waves, the calm inner centre of the sea where there is rest and clarity.

We are invited to listen, to meet people where they are at. Many times, it will be about listening to the wild storms that are currently erupting in their lives. However, as much as we meet people on the crest of the wave that is threatening their identity, security, etc., we can hold an inner posture with our own hearts that is from the depths of the sea. We know that the wave won't destroy their identity; their identity is deeper than that, even if they're unaware of it. We can't tell them this but we can *hold the inner knowing of it*, and gently, ever so gently, invite them on a journey of dropping down, dropping in, falling through the waves, and letting go of being rescued. Perhaps, in the letting go, they'll find that inner stillness that is their soul. When someone tastes this connection with the truth of their being, they can begin the long journey back home and learn the art of "staying close to themselves."

Our Need for Patience

It may take years of meeting the same person at a similar wave crest. As Spiritual Directors, we may become impatient. *Haven't we been here before? Haven't they "got it" yet?* When I become impatient, I reflect on the grace and kindness of those that met me over and over and over again in my places of challenge. Tears come even now as I remember the patience and gentleness that met me as I circled back time and time again with the same issues until, like water on a rock, the formation slowly emerged.

With tenderness and humility, I seek to remain present and let go of judgement of another life. In these moments, as Spiritual Directors, we are invited to *stay close to ourselves*. What if someone remains in a difficult place for a long time? Can I let go of how this session turns out, staying close to my own self, thus being able to be present to them without conditions? Over and over, we are invited to this *way of being*. And it is from our own deep living of this way that we can invite those we sit with to come and walk with us.

Tears come even now
as I remember the patience and gentleness
that met me
as I circled back
time and time again
with the same issues until,
like water on a rock,
the formation slowly emerged.

Practices of Returning to Oneself

It's been my experience that the fruit of getting hooked is self-doubt and loss of energy. The fruit of staying close to myself is trust and clarity of vision. So how does one stay close to oneself? There are perhaps many ways or spiritual practices that help you stay close to yourself, but

I'd like to offer six ways that have been significant in my own life and have become places of *return*.

1. *Rest*—I believe rest is a high spiritual practice that helps us reorient back to truth. Rest is like the waves of the ocean retreating after the extension to the shore. We need both the outward motion of action and the inward motion of stillness. Without both, we are unhealthy. Creating rest nurtures the soul, allowing time to become aware of our interior landscape. Rest provides opportunity for us to integrate the fullness of our experiences instead of becoming burnt out and disconnected.

2. *Beauty*—Beauty heals us. In a fractured world, especially when we're putting ourselves in the position of listening to others and exposing ourselves to trauma and pain, it's important to fill our lives with beauty. Beauty comes in so many forms: poetry, music, nature, fabric, and landscape. Being intentional about noticing beauty and allowing beauty to touch us every day reminds us of the beauty of our souls. Beauty touches something deep within us, reminding us of goodness, of hope, of love. The beauty of a rose can impact a room. The beauty of a song can heal the heart. Beauty is a spiritual quality that is ineffable. True beauty carries an essence that calls to the soul, reminding us of what is eternal.

3. *Permission to Move Slowly*—Our world is moving quickly. For many of us, our identities get caught up in a fast rhythm of accomplishment. To move slowly may feel lazy or sluggish. However, I believe there are times when it is holy and sacred to move slowly, to take time to make a cup of tea, to move gently as one gets dressed, to be intentional about writing a card. Moving slowly can help us become truly aware of the present moment, to really see what's before us without rushing to the next thing.

Moving slowly with a reading can help us become aware of a word or a phrase that we need to ponder, letting it sink in. Moving slowly on a walk can help us notice the turtles on the quiet log, and the trumpeter swans flying overhead on their way to the lake. Moving slowly can bring attentiveness that helps us return home to ourselves, to really see where we are and become present.

4. *Permission to Listen*—Permission. I have needed to give myself permission to truly listen to myself, my thoughts, my emotions, and my body's wisdom. Much of my life was about being more aware of others' thoughts, emotions, and physical needs rather than listening to my own. I have had to learn to become a friend to myself. This hasn't been easy, as listening to my deepest self has meant learning to tell the truth—to myself and to others. However, learning to listen has provided a sense of inner integrity and groundedness. But I had to give myself permission. Permission to truly listen *without editing and blaming*. And as I listened, I learned to return home and stay close to myself.

5. *Gazing*—What do we look at? I believe this is such an important aspect of staying close to ourselves. When I get hooked, it's because my gaze is on a circumstance or another person to provide something I want or need. Returning my gaze to inner Wisdom reorients me to truth. Being aware of where I'm putting my energy helps me to focus. It's like food—what I eat is what I become. What I gaze upon is who/what I reflect.

6. *Tenderness*—This word has been a spiritual discipline for me, shaping me and calling to me. I have found that Love, even when I'm facing painful truths, is profoundly tender. This tenderness, when I open to it, is what heals me and reorients me home, the place of deepest belonging. There's a kindness in being tender.

Love is not harsh or judgmental. Love speaks truth but holds the quality of healing and welcome home. *Tenderness is the touch of Love.*

The fruit of getting hooked is self-doubt and loss of energy. The fruit of staying close to myself is trust and clarity of vision.

Chapter XI

The Foundation of Love

To build a practice of any kind, there must be a foundation, a core, a centre from which we live, from which we offer our presence. Perhaps this is something we each need to take time to consider: What is my foundation? What are my core beliefs from which I am present to others?

I will offer to you what has become life-giving to me as I serve other souls.

I am a soul.
I come from Love, made by Love, going home to Love.
The human journey is one where I may have forgotten the truth of my being, but through Love's invitation, I move towards being remembered, returned, and restored.
As I turn to another being ...
I see a soul before me, full of infinite beauty.
I seek to bear witness to this soul, to honour and serve the truth that it bears.
I trust Love ... this soul comes from Love and is going home to Love.
Love is the healer, restorer, truth-teller, life-giver for this soul.
I am in service to Love; in Love I live and move and have my being.
Love undergirds all things.

Infinite Beauty in Others

One thing I have learned in moments where I'm truly present to the soul of another is that each one is full of infinite beauty. The truth of our being is usually covered over with a great deal of slime and yuck, lies and shame, guilt and remorse. But if we gently lift these layers, bit by bit the shining begins to come through, and the radiance of a soul starts to emerge. It may take years, but I truly believe it's possible and is the longing of the soul to be free to shine. It's the glory of being human.

It's paramount to hold this understanding of the significance, the beauty, the worth of the soul. People come to us and we see their personalities, their clothing, their outer drama, and we can get caught up in it. Often, it's all people know of themselves! We're devoting ourselves to something that they don't even know they carry within—the element of utmost glory, their soul. We become like those who are looking for buried treasure. We see all the piles of dirt, but we know that deep within is a radiant beauty yearning to live. We, as spiritual caregivers, are invited to care for and treat others with the value of their soul *already alive in our hearts*, even if it's not alive in their hearts.

Infinite Beauty in Ourselves

How can we see the beauty in others if we don't see it in ourselves? Our *first work* is to receive, over and over, how Love is revealing this truth to us! We are souls of infinite worth and beauty. We come from Love and are made by Love, going home to Love. As we begin to receive the truth of our souls, we can hold this truth for others. We're invited to become like children and receive the wild and expansive love that is always toward us, without fail—even when we're unaware.

To hold deep spaces for others
means that we need to learn
how to receive
over and over and over again.

We cannot hold space for others with small containers, and the only way we build a big container in ourselves is to receive the gifts that Love is bestowing on us and be expanded, transformed by grace.

Posture of Receptivity Key to Inner Transformation

How do we become people who know how to receive? I believe that transformation is primarily about a *posture of receptivity*. Transformation is not about attaining. It's about opening our hands to receive a grace. We're invited to hold within an *inner spaciousness* for Mystery to engage with our beings. This spaciousness is holy, sacred, and precious. This posture invites me to receive the truth of my value and the reality that I am a vessel of Love to flow through.

When I know the truth of my value, I am invited to stand tall with dignity. At the same time, I open my life in a posture of trust. Receiving love actually speaks to my dignity and worth. *I am worthy of receiving this love.* Knowing this changes *everything.*

As I learn to receive this love in my soul, my cup fills. I no longer need to know this through a human exchange, I know it in my soul. Receptivity to the truth of my being in Love sets the groundwork for any love I may be privileged to extend to another. The more my love flows to others from the unconditional love of the Divine, the purer and more fragrant this love will be. My spiritual practise is to turn again and again to receive the love my own heart needs from the Infinite. This is my source, my wellspring, my all.

Bearing Witness

If infinite beauty is about the value of a soul, bearing witness is about my *posture* to that soul. Bearing witness may perhaps seem passive or weak—a posture where not much saving action or fixing takes place. However, when one understands that the soul is infinitely beautiful, there's a liberation experienced for the listener as well as the one being listened to.

The Spiritual Director becomes one who helps to *see what is hidden*; one who notices and sheds light on what is happening. She is one who bears witness, reflecting back a mirrored image so the soul can begin to catch a glimpse of itself.

The soul is often like a beautiful swan looking in a mud-filled lake and seeing itself with great distortion. The listening companion is one who can be like clear water, creating a spaciousness for the muck and debris to be lifted and allowing a beauty to emerge. Bearing witness relieves the Spiritual Director of managing the problems of the directee and rather invites the directee to become aware of the inner movements of the heart and be in alignment with the truth of the soul in her/his life. This awareness will directly impact all the details of what is currently happening in the directee's life.

> *The spiritual director is one*
> *who bears witness,*
> *reflecting back a mirrored image*
> *so the soul can begin*
> *to catch a glimpse of itself.*

Trusting Love, Love Is the Healer

As I listen to others, the listening is based on a foundation of trust in Love. Love knows this person's story more than I ever will. Love undergirds this life and is attentive to things I will never understand. I am not the healer. I am not the fixer. I am not the magician. I am the one attentive, trusting that we are listening together to Love to guide the conversation, the way in which a life may unfold before us. This trust becomes a posture of the heart, a rich foundation so that the Spiritual Director may be in a place of rest and rootedness.

I Am in Service to Love

More than being in service to a person, I am service to Love. My intention is to serve in the way of Love. My first devotion is to fidelity: faithfulness to my own soul and to Love. This frees me from being in service to a *person* and the inner drive to make another happy, content, satisfied, etc. I hope the one I'm sitting with will feel all these things but the foundation of my vocation is service to Love. This means being okay with boundaries, speaking the truth, knowing my limitations, etc. My commitment is to be in integrity with my soul. This is foundational with every meeting, every conversation, every moment of every day. Even more than being in service to Love, I see my whole life as immersed in this Love—*in Love I live, I move, and have my being.* Prayer is to help me remember the truth of this.

Love Undergirds All Things

Even with the best of intentions, prayer practices, and spiritual disciplines, I will fail. I won't always love as purely as I desire. I won't live up to all the ideals of my life. I'll let people down. However, there is a peace that lives in me, that Love is greater than my failings. I know that I may disappoint, but Love is more expansive than me. Love undergirds my shadows, my shortcomings, my failings. I commit those I love to Love and pray that this is ultimately what they know deep in their hearts: that their lives are undergirded by a Love that is much more than I will ever have for them, and that this Love is the ground of their being. This is the Love I can rest in and then dare to have the courage to listen to their beautiful souls.

Soul Prayer

Beauty to enfold me
Mercy to surround me
Truth to fill me
Hope to ignite me

Peace in my sleeping
Flow in my waking
Joy in my trusting
Faith in my waiting

Firmness in my standing
Living water in my dancing
Holy Breath in my soul
Living Fire in my heart

The Living Presence in my ever-living soul
The Living Presence in my ever-living soul

Cathy AJ Hardy

Chapter XII

Rooted in Silence—Nurtured by Love

When I began receiving Spiritual Direction in 1998, I entered a period of three years that became the most formative years of my life, but I didn't see those years as formational at the time. I was just surviving, in pain, and in my perspective, barely making it. But in those three years, I was introduced to Spiritual Direction, the music of Taizé, silent retreats, labyrinths, and the rhythms of a contemplative life. Each of these elements made a huge impact on me and invited me to develop an inner spirituality of receiving soul nourishment where once I had known a parched and desert wasteland. I didn't know it then, but all these elements played a part in creating the "School of Formation", a pathway of transformation that taught me the lessons foundational in spiritual formation and spiritual direction.

Silence, the First Step of "In and Down" to the Roots

I remember the first time I experienced five minutes of silence while participating in a group studying meditation and contemplation. It was horribly uncomfortable. Strange. Like eating a foreign food that felt odd in my mouth. I wasn't sure about it. I didn't like feeling disoriented. I didn't like being with myself in a quiet way. However, a week or so later, I realized that those five minutes had done something to me and for me. The silence lit a candle inside of myself in a space that I hadn't realized was even there. I became hungry for more. Over those three formative years, I deepened into longer periods of silence, some alone and some shared in a group. I didn't understand what was happening, only that an inner thirst was being ignited.

Spiritual Direction was something I began to receive in these years, and Joy was introducing me to the art of silence through her posture toward me. Our times were saturated in silence. As uncomfortable as it made me, I realized that there were small things I was becoming aware of *because of the silence*. I became more aware of the words I was saying and the words Joy was saying to me. Our conversations became slow and filled with attentiveness and thoughtfulness.

> *Our conversations became slow*
> *and filled with attentiveness*
> *and thoughtfulness.*

There was no need to rush an answer to a question. There was value in being truthful. As a result, I became more attentive when I was in conversations with others. *What were they really saying? What was I really saying? Were my words even true? Did my words match my intention?* I realized how out of sorts I truly was. I realized how many mistruths I spoke every day because I wasn't connected with myself. Joy's silence bore fruit in my life in countless ways.

Joy was the one who sent me on my first silent retreat. I was so nervous, but what a gift she gave me. I will always be thankful. As I drove from Atlanta to the south of Georgia to this retreat, I was very apprehensive. What would I do over three days without talking, except for one hour each day during Spiritual Direction? How could I handle hanging out with myself and being in silence? Even though that retreat happened more than twenty years ago, I can still see it clearly in my mind. I remember feeling a little lost and confused, wandering the grounds and not really knowing what to do with myself. However, the gifts that came through that journey were ones I unpacked for years to come and continue to unpack now. I recognized in the months following this first retreat that silence created a holy sanctuary within. I learned that if I had the courage to yield to the silence, there were profound gifts that would continue giving, becoming consolation that would lead to even more consolation.

Taizé and the Labyrinth

The music of Taizé was introduced to me during that three-year period as well. Taizé is an ecumenical community that was founded in Southern France in 1940 by a Swiss man, Brother Roger. During WWII, Brother Roger used his property as a safe place for those needing refuge. After the war, he developed a community of prayer, song, and service. Over the years, it became a gathering place, especially for young people, who would come by the thousands every summer for prayer, song and conversation. Brother Roger's heart was that we would sing our prayers, and he developed intentional ways of doing this. The form of song that emerged was rooted in simplicity: one or two lines of a thought, truth, or scripture set to a beautiful melody that would become a meditation, an inner mantra of the heart. Taizé became known as a place of rich spiritual fellowship through the practice of song.

A dear friend, Christina, who had visited the Taizé community, had handed me a small booklet of Taizé music. She told me that I should lead the local church, where we both attended, with these songs. I thought that was a crazy request. But I went home, sat at the piano, and began to learn the small meditative chants of Taizé. In a surprising way, the melodies and words began to captivate my heart. I had been praying in my solitude; "God, my life is so dark ... I feel so dark!" One of the songs that I learned from that little booklet held these words from Psalm 139: "The darkness is never darkness in your sight; the deepest night is clear as the daylight."[12] I felt stunned. *Could it be that*

....

12   Chants de Taizé (Taizé–Communauté, France: Ateliers et Presses de Taizé, 1999), 25

my darkness did not look dark in the eyes of Love? Could it be that my own understanding was limited? Could it be that Love's view was expansive, and that my darkness was held in light? These were questions that began to fill me as I meditated on this song and others from Taizé.

The labyrinth also became a tool of growth and awareness. I was skeptical of it at first. What is this maze-like path? Why would anyone walk this? What strange thing could this be? But Christina, the same friend who had handed me the book of Taizé songs, was enthusiastic about the labyrinth, and she was impossible to say no to. I *had* to walk it. And so, I did. The labyrinth began to be one of my teachers. As I started the labyrinth path for the first time, I wanted to walk right to the centre; however, the labyrinth guided me left. And then right. And then left again, and then in circles. I had to let go of my carefully laid plans and surrender to a path. Over and over and over. The labyrinth became a symbol of letting go and trusting what I didn't know. I had to surrender what I thought I knew and be open to where the path would lead me. I will always be grateful to Christina for bringing the music of Taizé and the journey of the labyrinth to me.

Contemplative Living

All of these experiences profoundly affected my soul and brought me into a contemplative way of living. I didn't know it at the time, but they were like nutrients to my soil, allowing the roots of my tree to be able to travel down deep and drink living water. I slowly began to live in a way I had never lived before: rooted and listening, attentive and present. Even though my life situation hadn't changed, and what was difficult remained, I was changing inside. I couldn't see it at first, but over time, my tree began to bear fruit.

It wasn't necessarily any one of these experiences mentioned above, but together, these contemplative elements taught me a way to walk. Contemplation taught me to slow down, pay attention, listen, notice, speak with intention, rest, trust, yield, surrender, open to grace, and so much more.

Contemplation taught me to slow down,
pay attention,
listen, notice, speak with intention,
rest, trust, yield, surrender,
open to grace,
and so much more.

From developing a contemplative awareness, I began to receive gifts of healing and grace in my soul. Old wounds were healing, and my inner and outer posture began to change. The desert wasteland was turning to a rich, dark soil that my roots were responding to. I began to listen to my soul and live in alignment with Love in growing ways. I began to see my value and worth as well as the worth and value of those around me. This changed the trajectory of my life, and I tasted joy for the first time.

The interesting thing about this contemplative way is that when one truly receives and transforms, there is a sense of outflow that eventually emerges. When Love is the source, Love heals, restores, deepens the roots ... and then overflows. Love is never meant to be kept in a bottle. Love is expansive and generative. There are times in one's life when one may need to be on the receiving end for quite some time. But when that Love is truly received, there's a joy that rises up and one longs to share with another out of the wild overflow that emerges in time. A desire grew in my heart to share with others what had become, and continues to this day, to be so life-giving for me. I learned to live into Brother Roger's words: "Are we not called to communicate a mystery of hope to those around us by the lives we lead?"[13]

------

13   Friends of Silence, accessed July 14, 2020, https://friendsofsilence.net/quote/source/thin-places

Are we not called to communicate
a mystery of hope
to those around us
by the lives we lead?

Br. Roger of Taize

Contemplation—Our Life as a Tree

I believe that a life of contemplation is like the life of a tree. It's the journey *in and down* ... first. Contemplation is deepening of one's root system into the soil and further yet into the inner-wellsprings before the fruit emerges on a branch. This journey *in and down* is a hidden and silent journey, often with a great deal of solitude of the heart. It can be confusing like a labyrinth and disorienting at times. The places of our formation may be dark and obscure to our sight. However, the darkness of our inner soil is not dark to Love; it shines as the daylight. In this place, as we are held and nurtured in Love, we are meant, like a seed in the ground, to let go of the form we've known. We are invited to surrender into the process of yielding our shell to the earth, opening and expanding into the darkness. A seed needs to be in the darkness before it can spring into the light. A seed needs to go down before it goes up. *And so, must we.*

Contemplative practices and ways of living help us to go down, creating an inner spaciousness of the heart. I believe we must be at home with the journey of in and down, because that is the place of transformation. Few will go here alone, so the gift of Spiritual Direction is one of accompaniment into the soil of another, into the darkness of a life, knowing a tree is being born.

In
and
down

Silent and hidden...

Contemplative practices root us in silence,
allowing our own tree
to be fed continually by Love,
even as we are present to others.

Contemplative practices root us in silence, allowing our own tree to be fed continually by Love, even as we are present to others. Storms may come and go in our lives, but our root system is what holds us steady. Being rooted in silence and contemplative living grounds us as we are present to our very lives and those we listen to.

Expanding Outwards—Vulnerability and Tenderness

One of the first things I did with sharing out of what I had received was to create evenings of song with the music of Taizé. I loved creating nights where we could sing and sing and sing. I knew what these songs were doing for me, and I longed to share them with others and have them experience the grace of light in their darkness. Over time, I began to also facilitate silent retreats, and the work of Soul Care began to grow and take on a life of its own.

When I first began to share out of my heart from the overflow of what I had received, I would feel quite vulnerable and naked afterwards. I was sharing something so new and tender within me. It was also new and different for those in my community, especially when I came back home to B.C., Canada. My family and friends didn't know this language of contemplation and stillness, so as I began to share of these life-giving tools, I wasn't always understood. I was filled with passion but was also vulnerable.

These things were still new for me, and my own roots were still rather fragile. My old pattern was to look to others for affirmation and approval. Would my offerings to others be met with appreciation and recognition? Would I be understood and acknowledged? I soon came to face the fact that there was something deeper motivating me. I so deeply desired to share what I had been given, so even though I knew I'd be often misunderstood, I chose to do it anyways.

Continued Nurture in Our Roots—Love in Our Vulnerability

This inner resolve brought peace to my heart; however, I realized I had a need to know if I was on track. One night as I was driving home after a beautiful evening of sung prayers, I called out to the Holy One: "How was the evening in your eyes?" I was about to drive over a bridge that crosses the beautiful Fraser River close to my home. As I crossed the bridge, I had a most ineffable experience. I felt Love surround my vehicle and sing to me. It seemed there was a myriad of angels and beings I could not name that encircled me. I remember it clearly to this day. There was a knowing of deep love and celebration for the evening. I experienced feeling affirmed and seen through this encounter as I drove over the bridge. I could go home in peace, not looking for affirmation from another, but rooted in Divine Love's presence with me.

This experience became a pattern in my life after I would share my heart with others. After many events as I would travel home and cross the bridge, I would turn to Love. "How did you see this experience?" And I would receive Love's presence and words in my life. How I cherish these memories. How these moments fed my soul. Love's words to me became the most important of my life. In moments when I felt self-doubt or confusion, I would reach out for perspective, understanding, and direction. The roots of my tree received the greatest nourishment when I would return to the contemplative practices of stillness, listening, and attentiveness to Divine Love. I had to turn to my Source, *not to those I was serving*, for continued nourishment and growth.

Integration with Spiritual Direction—Turning to Love

Years later, as I began to offer Spiritual Direction as part of the overall Soul Care work, I realized this practice of turning to Love after a session was so important. I wanted to know that a session had gone well for the directee, but there were many times when it was impossible to know. Sometimes people left in a quiet way. Other times people were overwhelmed with the depths of where we had travelled and wanted to hold their thoughts inside. They were letting it all still settle when they left. At times I wondered if I had said too much, too little, or the wrong thing. I struggled with self-doubt. Turning to Love after a session became like the drive home over the bridge. Sometimes I needed affirmation. Sometimes I needed direction. Other times I asked if I needed correction. I'd sit in silence and turn my heart toward Love. And wait. Peace would come as I would take time to listen, to receive, to understand. Instead of looking for affirmation from what I could see directly through evidence in the work, my affirmation was coming from Love.

Our Roots as Spiritual Companions

To receive my worth, my value, my affirmation from Love has rooted and grounded me many times when I was unsteady. There have been so many challenging situations that have made me unsure of myself. It would have been easy to project what "might be going on" and to speculate on what the directee "might be experiencing" from our time together. To go to Love helped me *stay close to myself* and stay grounded in truth rather than in my fear.

There is so much we don't know as we offer loving space for others in Spiritual Direction, and we need to know where our roots are. Drinking deeply from the wellsprings of life will restore us again and again and again. We all need input, feedback, affirmation, and approval. But where do we get it? Where are we looking for it? Where is our gaze? As Spiritual Directors, we need to return to our Source over and over again. We need to turn to the One for whom even the darkness shines as the daylight. Our fears, anxieties, and longings can all be so deeply met as we turn toward the Love from which we came.

I invite you to find your own practice as you give from your heart to another. What do you look for when you have given to another? What does your heart need to know? What does your heart need to hear?

What does your heart need to know?
What does your heart need to hear?

You may be depleted, tired, and worn out after listening to another soul. Love knows what you need, and there's no shame in this. You are Love's partner as you are loving others, so you can turn to your Source and know that it isn't too much to ask for what you need.

Rooted in Silence—Nourished by Love

I believe that when we sit with another in Spiritual Direction, our presence is what sets the tone in the room. When we have allowed our roots to deepen through contemplation, we carry the qualities of our stillness and silence in our listening, in our attentiveness, in our ability to be fully present. Rooted in silence, we create a container for grace and encounter. Rooted in silence, we rest in knowing our identity in Love. Rooted in silence, we receive the continued nourishment for our own souls and are thus able to give from the overflow of this abundance.

Chapter XIII

Projections—Stand in One Place

Projections are slippery, elusive energies that are challenging to deal with because they emerge from our unconscious. They hold such power because we are totally unaware of how our behaviour is manifesting an element of our shadow. As we receive Spiritual Direction, our work is to turn toward our shadow sides and allow illumination where possible to bring greater integration from our unconscious into our consciousness. As we offer Spiritual Direction, we will still continue working with our own shadows. Hopefully, we can also recognize those moments when a directee is projecting their shadows onto us.

My Struggles with Projections

When I first began to see Joy, she felt like an attractive motherly figure to me. My relationship with my own mother had been fraught with challenges, and there was a deep longing in me (although I wasn't aware of it at the time) to be mothered in a way that felt nurturing and safe. In some ways, there was a little girl in me that longed to be held and cared for by a maternal figure. I longed for approval and affirmation and acceptance from my own mother and unconsciously projected those longings onto Joy. This is not a bad longing. It's a natural human longing and need. However, it was unconscious on my part. Instead of facing my own inner pain regarding this and working toward healing, I projected onto Joy the mother role and hoped that she would fulfill my needs.

The projection held positive and negative aspects. It was a positive projection in that I esteemed Joy and held her in high regard. It was negative in that I unconsciously wanted her to meet my unconscious emotional needs. I put her on a pedestal to the point of not seeing her as a person. I know that Joy experienced "feeling" my projections, my devotion to her, and also my emotional pull for her to meet the longings of my heart.

What I didn't know then but know now is that Joy skillfully held her ground, not succumbing to my grandiose vision of her and also not bending over backwards to accommodate my needs. She was steady. She was calm. The way she responded actually rattled me. I was used to a certain dance of relationship with the women of my family, and I assumed the "dance position" with Joy. She didn't dance the dance. I panicked. I didn't know how to have a relationship of healthy boundaries and clear communication. I was used to manipulation and evasive emotional coercion. Confusing conversation was normal. Straightforward communication scared me.

I projected onto Joy all of the female forms of relationship I had known, and she remained still. Over time, I realized that Joy was modelling something new for me to learn. It was a bumpy road, but slowly over those three years, I learned about boundaries and about integrity in relationship. Through her example, Joy became the first woman I knew where I experienced a freedom I had never known before—a freedom to actually discover my own thoughts and be myself. It was extraordinary. I eventually let go of my unhealthy projections toward Joy and came to experience something healing and freeing in the relationship that has impacted every relationship since.

Projections Are Mirrors of the Inner Life

Projections can come in many forms. When we're on the receiving end of them, we might be tempted to be puffed up by someone's delight in us, or we might be tempted to be devasted by someone's disdain. A projection has nothing to do with us. It's about the deep, internal work that is happening in those we are with. It's likely completely unconscious on their part, just as it was for me with Joy at the beginning of our Spiritual Direction relationship. However, because Joy stayed neutral, I was able to recognize it over time. If she had allowed herself to get caught in the projection and played a role as "mother" to me, we would have both become lost. It took great strength on her part to recognize what was happening and hold steady. It took time for me to face my shadows and become conscious in that area of my life and release the grip of this projection.

As people act out, both positively and negatively, we can learn to notice what might be happening. It can be hard to put a finger on it, as it's elusive. But there's usually an energy that one feels. Instead of taking it personally, it's wise to just notice what's happening through taking time to be still. Sometimes I actually push away the air in front of me and talk to the projection when I'm alone, letting it loosen its tentacles. A projection can feel like a spider's web descending, or a tantalizing temptation. My work is to be kind and hold the directee with love, knowing that this is something that reflects their inner work. To not take things personally, both positively and negatively, requires much attentiveness and willingness on our part to face our own shadows and what might hook us out of ourselves.

Getting Hooked by Projections

We all have our weak areas when a projection occurs. Whatever is unconscious in us can be triggered into a reaction by a projection. This is where a lifestyle of stillness and listening, being rooted and grounded, makes all the difference in the world. There's an inner stillness that can alert me that something is amiss and I need to pay attention. Of course, I don't always catch these red flags and can be utterly hooked. But the more we become conscious of it, the more we can notice things as they are occurring and respond from a depth of love and truth.

My own weak area is that I can tend to feel overly responsible for people, so when a directee is projecting onto me their need of a rescuer and saviour, I can get hooked into that role. Love's work in me is to stay present to others without biting that bait. I've learned I can be compassionate and present without rescuing. This saves me from burnout, emotional fatigue, and the sense of being overwhelmed. Our work, although deep and rich, isn't meant to be heavy. When we're feeling a heaviness over a long period of time, it may be helpful to ask what projections we've absorbed that are not rooted in truth.

Stand in One Place

One of Doreen's sayings that comes out of her meditation with the proverbs of the Desert Abbas and Ammas is a helpful guide as we deal with projections or anything else that might pull us out of ourselves: "Stand in one place. Stand where your heart is rooted in Love. And God will live in the action."[14]

"Stand in one place.
Stand where your heart is rooted in Love.
And God will live in the action."

Doreen Kostynuik

....

14   Doreen Kostynuik, "Standing in Place—Acting in Love", CaravanVol 15. No 61, 6–7.

Stand in one place

Rooted in Love

Love will do the action

This saying is again one of an inner posture, of standing. When a projection comes, we're pulled out of ourselves in a response that is not rooted in Love. Love invites us to stand, to stand where we are deeply rooted. I believe the more we do our work, the more we'll come to greater awareness of the energy in our bodies. When we're pulled out of ourselves, there's a forward type of energy that feels like we are pushing, striving, controlling, fixing, etc. This is a reactive energy rooted in anxiety and fear, and it does not bear healthy fruit in our lives. To stand in one place means an inner posture of rest, stillness, silence, and equanimity. When our *response* to others comes out of *standing in one place*, it's flowing out of Love. Love is then the action, and this action bears rich fruit. Responding in love is so different than reacting in fear. Reacting usually means a lack of consciousness; it is quick and often protective. When we respond from rooted love, we don't need to protect anything. We can move from a place of wholeness and wellbeing.

No matter the projection, we are invited to stand in one place, stand where our hearts are rooted in Love. This is our place of freedom and choice. We can choose how to respond, even if we're tempted to be hooked. The difference is that we become conscious of the projection and we can, in stillness, listen for wisdom and respond from a place of freedom.

Chapter XIV

Questions to Unlock the Door

*"Asking the proper question is the central action of transformation—
in fairy tales, in analysis, and in individuation.
The key question causes germination of consciousness.
The properly shaped question always emanates from an essential curiosity
about what stands behind.
Questions are the keys that cause the secret doors of the
psyche to swing open."*

Dr. Clarissa Pinkola Estes[15]

From Answers to Questions

Early on in my Spiritual Direction experience, I was impacted by the questions Joy would ask me. I had grown up as a pastor's daughter in a small community in British Columbia, Canada. I was drilled with *answers*. It was my job to know the answers. Answers were a part of my very identity. However, as I sat broken-hearted in Spiritual Direction, Joy asked questions of me that I couldn't easily respond to. I found

---

15   Clarissa Pinkola Estes, Ph.D., Women Who Run with the Wolves (New York: Ballantine Books, 1992), 52.

myself stumped with confusion, hit by flashes of awareness, and floundering for words. Sometimes these questions made me feel exposed, as though they revealed a mask I didn't even know I was wearing. I felt vulnerable and tender. These questions were probing into my very soul, and even as they undid me, they opened the ground of my soil so that I could receive the seed of truth.

The Art of Asking a Soul Question

The art of asking a soul-evoking question, I learned over time, creates space for the individual to spiral inside of themselves and enter the woods of their own being. To receive more answers and dogma would have lined the bookshelves of my mind and provided me with a sense of accomplishment (even though false) that I understood the inner workings of my soul. What Joy did so craftily was to use a question to make me do the hard work of entering the woods, finding my way through the brambles, tangles, and broken pieces of my life.

As a Spiritual Director, asking questions of this nature is my hard work when sitting with another. It's easy for me to want to give answers, especially when the directee would also love my "profound wisdom," my "glorious thoughts," and my "perfect guidance" for their lives. How my pride can sneak into the room. How we both want the easy way. If I tell you what you want me to say, I'll feel good, and you'll feel good. However, neither of us will grow. Neither of us will have been faithful to our souls and the intention of our meeting. I too, as a Spiritual Director, must attune to the deeper questions of our meeting. I must drop down underneath the waves, under the intensity, under the emotions, under the drama ... and listen. What are questions that can open the door? What are the questions that move beyond facts and turn toward motivations, yearnings, hidden truths?

What are questions
that move beyond facts
and turn toward motivations,
yearnings, hidden truths?

As I am listening to someone share what's on their heart, I listen attentively. Then, if and when possible, I invite us to pause so I can listen more deeply. These are the basic questions that I attend to *in myself* as I listen for further questions to ask the one I am with.

Questions for Myself as I Listen

+ *What am I aware of now?*
+ *What is the energy/emotion in the room (striving, pushing, longing, grieving, disappointment, anger)?*
+ *As I drop down, what do I notice?*
+ *What is Love's invitation in the midst of this? For me? For the directee?*
+ *How can I hold the posture of this invitation in a question?*

Questions Arising Out of Listening

Out of listening and asking my own heart questions, I can attune to a question to ask the one before me. My whole practice is filled with questions: questions for my heart, questions for Love, questions for the directee. Part of the joy of asking questions that come from the depths of listening, rooted in Love, is the wonder of the journey that the directee begins to understand. They begin to listen to their heart. They begin to hear the whisper of Love. They begin to catch a glimpse of their diamond soul. They begin to know that their heart carries a wisdom that can guide their lives. Their countenance begins to shift. They stand a little taller. They speak their truth more clearly. Over time, they find their way home.

Paul

I'm not a Spiritual Director for Paul, but a friend. However, Paul wrote me an e-mail, and a form of Spiritual Direction conversation emerged. Paul wrote and expressed frustration about an event he had experienced, one he'd been excited for. I could hear disappointment underneath his words. As I pondered his communication and allowed myself to feel his angst, these questions arose in me: What were the hopes? What were the disappointments? What was the longing? What does that tell you about yourself? What is Love inviting you to through this awareness? This is Paul's response in his own words:

"When Cathy first responded to my email and I saw the questions she had sent, I thought, "Are you kidding me? I don't want to look at any of this. I just want to forget it all." I left them alone but they percolated in me all day, so I finally looked at them again and knew I needed to journal with the answers that were sitting in me. It was easy to list my hopes, disappointments, and longings; they were surface and strong.

Then came the question: "What does that tell you about yourself?" Again, I thought, "Are you kidding me? Tell about me? Nothing." Oh, but I was so wrong. Here's where the heart started opening up, and depths beyond the event surfaced. Images of myself seemed to flash before me, and deeper truths I knew I need to explore within my prayer and with my Spiritual Director arose.

The beauty and struggle of it all came with the final question: "What is Love inviting you to through this awareness?" I was able to quickly let go of the frustrations with the event I had experienced, as they served only as a launching point. Love was inviting me into new awareness of how I was walking in my faith journey, but also of long-time truths I needed to become reacquainted with so to hear Love's voice more clearly."

Myths and Legends—Tools for Asking Questions

Jungian psychology is a tremendous tool in Spiritual Direction, with the vast wealth of symbolism and metaphor that is so highly valued in this discipline. Carl Jung honoured images, dreamwork, and story in the understanding of the soul journey. Our lives are stories that are full of characters and symbols. When we begin to pay attention to the stories that people are telling us, we can use these characters and symbols as platforms for very profound questions that may unlock a mystery of their journey. The more we understand myths, legends, ancient symbols, and characters, the more we can incorporate these into the very questions we ask.

Sally

As I sat with Sally in a Spiritual Direction session, we took time for silence after she had shared her heart. To my surprise, the image of Cinderella came to my mind in the silence. I held that image in my heart as I pondered all that this person had shared. I then asked her: "I wonder what it was like for Cinderella to be hidden when she knew who she truly was?" We had never spoken of this fairy tale before. This moment surprised her. Sally told me that she hadn't thought of that story since she was a teenager. It was a story that had resonated with her at that time in her life. We then explored, in the same way we would explore a dream, what symbolism this story might hold.

Here are some of Sally's reflections in her own words:

Cathy honoured what I shared by holding it in a moment of silence. When she ended the silence, she expressed a wondering about Cinderella and if there are themes that could be drawn out of both stories. Initially I was startled at her question. There were moments as a teenager when I felt I could connect with Cinderella's character, but I brushed them off as "childish pity thoughts" and wouldn't entertain them.

Having Cathy bring up this story allowed me to validate my past con-
nection with the tale and the associated feelings of hurt. The complexity of
the story has allowed for me to sit with the struggle of Cinderella's early
life. Cinder means ashes, so what are the ashes in my life? What was it like
for Cinderella to be hidden and unseen by those around her? She found
unexpected friendship in the mice. Who are the mice and areas of joy in
my life?

But her story doesn't stop there. We could also walk with Cinderella
as she transitioned into a Queen and wonder how she would lead a
Queendom. I remember in that moment experiencing validity in my
feelings and hope for what the future can develop into. There are many
differences between Cinderella's story and mine; however, sitting with her
experience has allowed me to connect with deeper processes moving inside
of me.

If exploring the story with someone, here are some possible questions to ask. When asking questions, we pay attention to the questions
that spark an energy or an awareness.

- *What are the ashes in your life? (Cinder=ashes)*
- *What was it like for Cinderella to be hidden and unseen by those around her?*
- *Where did you feel hidden as a teenager?*
- *Where do you currently feel hidden?*
- *What is similar between that time past and the time now?*
- *Where do you currently feel exploited?*
- *What do you know in your heart of who you are?*
- *What are the choices you currently have as you respond to your situation?*
- *What is the invitation?*
- *What is the dress you are invited to wear?*
- *Who are the animals that Love has sent to encourage you?*

- *What is your inner inheritance that you can claim even if not seen by others?*
- *What is the 'Queendom' you are invited to know?*

A Question from Joy

One question that Joy asked me has stayed with me over twenty years: "What did Mary have to give up to say yes?" Using the stories of the Gospels, she would ask me a question that pertained to my own heart but also brought me out of my own story to identify with another. This question awakened my heart to the courage of Mary in letting go of how she thought her life would be to say yes to the life she actually had. Identifying with Mary through the gift of that question gave me the courage to say *yes* to my own life, even though it held crushing blows and broken dreams. Identifying with Mary allowed me to be open to the wonder and mystery of Love entering my story and guiding me to something bigger than what I could currently see. Stepping into a larger story expanded my life and helped me take the next steps.

When Joy asked that question, I had to turn *inwards*, explore the depths of my being, and find the inner courage to respond to what life was asking of me. I didn't know the answer to that question at first. In fact, I left the Spiritual Direction session discouraged because I didn't know. I wanted to know, but I didn't. I had to struggle. I had to wrestle. I had to be uncomfortable with the not knowing. But one day, an awareness bubbled in me. It blossomed like a rose in my heart. I knew. I knew and knew and knew. And then the answer filled me with a fragrance that I still carry to this day. The answer was my heart's discovery, not Joy's wisdom. The answer changed my life.

And then the answer
filled me with a fragrance that I still carry to this day.
The answer was my heart's discovery,
not Joy's wisdom.
The answer changed my life.

Questions Create Self-Discovery

When we're able to learn the art of asking questions, we allow others the opportunity to discover the truth, the wisdom, the courage, the wild pureness of their own souls. This is one of the greatest gifts we can give another. I'm still learning this art, but it's one of my goals to deepen into asking richer questions. In this way, I can stand at the door of mystery and witness another soul find the beauty and glory that is already there.

What is a question that has changed your life?
How did discovering the answer within impact you?

Chapter XV

Embracing Darkness and Solitude

There's an important aspect of deep soul work that is, like in many myths and legends from the past, similar to the heroine stepping into the dark woods alone. Two elements are necessary for the soul journey: embracing holy darkness and inner solitude.

Holy Darkness

Darkness is a word that has a deeply negative connotation in our vocabulary, often insinuating that darkness and evil are one. It's time to untangle these words and rediscover the gift and sacredness of darkness. Gertrud Muller Nelson, the author of *Here All Dwell Free*, told me that Disney, in its portrayal of many fairy tales, has contributed to our understanding of the "dark woods" being sinister in nature. However, she explained that in many of the older European myths and legends, the dark woods were the place of healing, restoration, and discovery. How can we open our understanding of darkness as it pertains to Spiritual Direction? I believe that the following three images can help us see darkness in a new light.

Darkness of the Womb

The womb is something we've all known but never seen. We've all experienced this place but we can't describe it or even remember all that those nine months held. We were in *formation*, the process of becoming. Formation of a new creation is often slow, hidden, mysterious, and dark. We can't measure it. We can't quantify it. We have to leave it alone and allow it to do something beyond what our minds understand. There's a deep intelligence at work in formation, but it's unquantifiable and intangible. The darkness of the womb is one of *preparing for birth*. If we cut short this process, invade or control it, we impact the new life trying to emerge.

There's something sacred about waiting, about not being in control of the process, about surrendering to the right timing, about allowing, about trusting the darkness of the womb in its mysterious work of creating.

There is something sacred about waiting,
about not being in control of the process,
about surrendering to the right timing,
about allowing,
about trusting the darkness of the womb
in its mysterious work of creating.

Many people come to Spiritual Direction who are "in the womb." And they want to get out … *early*. It isn't time yet. They're being held in the Great Mother's womb and are being formed in new ways. It's uncomfortable at times. They can't see. They can't know. They're invited to rest, to trust, to surrender to Love. I was in this place when I saw Joy, and I would say I re-entered the womb many times, as there was much more formation I was invited to know. However, in those beginning years, Joy became like a midwife to my soul, speaking to me and guiding me into a posture of trust and surrender when I was kicking and screaming. I hated not knowing. I hated not seeing. I hated the darkness. But Joy wasn't afraid of it. Joy invited me to surrender, to trust something larger than myself. I remember that day very clearly, a day when I actually chose to posture my body in a kneeling position and say yes. That "yes" became like the soothing lullaby that helped this unborn being rest and allowed the birth of me to unfold. It was long. It was slow. It was painful. But it was worth waiting for.

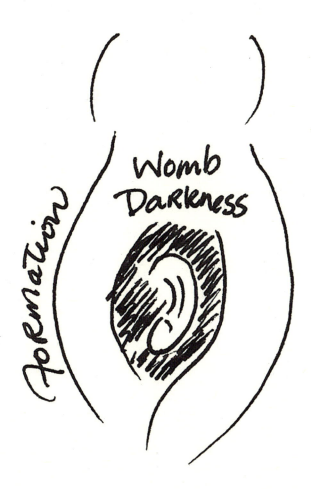

I hear the desire from many people to "do" Spiritual Direction correctly or to "get" contemplation. In those moments, I remember the years of formative darkness and how none of this can be measured in ways that are familiar to us. Spiritual Direction can be a platform for our birth, but our formation is a lifetime. We yield again and again and again. We don't "get it" in a weekend or an hour session. We're learning a way to walk. We're learning a way to trust. We're learning to embrace the seasons of darkness so that we can be reborn again and again and again into new life.

We're invited to accompany others in their places of not knowing. Our temptation may be to fill the empty spaces with words, to "fix" the embryo, to blaze into the womb with a torch of light. None of this is helpful for the formation of the soul. If we recognize that someone is in the womb of Love, our work is to come alongside and attend to the quiet and hidden places of darkness; speaking the words of a loving mid-wife, knowing that a soul is being formed.

Darkness of the Earth

When I moved back to British Columbia, I found that I lived very close to the opening of some beautiful woods. I began to walk there almost every day for a period of ten years. The woods became my friend, my teacher, my comfort. One of the aspects of the woods that fascinated me was the beautiful root systems of the red cedars, pines, and maples. Some roots you could hardly see at all as the tree would go straight down into the earth. But other roots would stretch horizontally and slip across the path under my feet. I would look down at these roots and then way, way up, not able to see the far reaches of the branches kissing the sky.

I became fascinated with these trees and their roots. One time I tucked myself in at the base of a tree to find comfort. Another time a grove of trees seemed to encircle me with protection. I lay my hands on their bark. I stood looking at these quiet giants with wonder. The trees became my teachers. I realized there was an aspect of them I could never "get my hands on" or know—their roots. They lived with their lives half-hidden, an inner place of receiving, nurture, and darkness. These trees taught me more than any book the reality of living a contemplative life and that the dark soil of silence and nurture is of utmost importance for the health and wellbeing of the tree. Darkness with the roots is hiddenness.

For those yielding to transformation, they are perhaps entering a "hidden" journey for the first time. They're turning inwards to their roots, acknowledging the places of their life that are full of mystery and not-knowing. Our work is to cultivate the soil of this precious tree and help create the atmosphere of silence and stillness that is under the ground of so much noise and business.

*Our work
is to cultivate the soil
of this precious tree
and to help create
the atmosphere of silence and stillness
that is under the ground
of so much noise and business.*

Darkness in the roots is about the journey in and down, to places where there are often no words or ways to explain. Being hidden is not a value in our society. We want recognition and acknowledgement. However, when we surrender to a hiddenness with our roots, we find the greatest recognition and acknowledgement of our lives. Our souls come home to the source of all: Love. It's a paradoxical journey, the one in and down. But what our hearts are truly longing for will be found in the richness of the deep earth, the wellspring of Love.

Darkness of the Chrysalis

The journey of the caterpillar into a butterfly is a truly astonishing alchemical resurrection of sorts. When the caterpillar enters the chrysalis, it loses all form. *All* form. Everything of how it has known itself to be is completely dissolved. There's absolutely no recognition left. The only thing that remains is cellular liquid. A caterpillar cell soup. *Mush*. And from this absolute breakdown of form and a season of darkness, a new life is created. True transformation is now possible.

The Greek word *entelechy* describes the intelligence that lies in each cell of this soup. Every cell carries the *entelechy* of a butterfly. The knowledge of its becoming is vibrantly waiting in the cells, even though completely without form. There is so much metaphor that one can explore with the journey of a butterfly. Out of her journey into mush, she resurrects into a new life form. When she first emerges, there is a fragility and tenderness to her. She needs to be very still and allow the sun to soak into her wings before she can take that first flight. Her new life becomes one of migration, of journey, of new beginnings.

Spiritual Direction can be a place and a season of a dark chrysalis, sitting with those whose worlds have completely left them destroyed, those who don't know who they are anymore, those who can't recognize any of their surroundings, as so much has been lost. Sometimes being in the chrysalis takes a very long time. The chrysalis journey is not a time to be talking about the possibilities of the butterfly. It's not a time to be talking about travel and new beginnings. It's a time to be with disorientation, loss, and confusion. It's a time of letting go, of yielding to being without form. This can be extremely painful, and times like this can require much gentleness, silence, and profound compassion.

It's only grace when one recognizes that the chrysalis is not forever. But one discovers that slowly, gently, and with a sense of surprise. The work of the *entelechy* of our souls is a grace to behold, but it's not a work we can control or manage. It's not our work to put a timeline on anyone's suffering. We're invited to hold the space of compassion during loss, grace in disorientation, kindness in grief.

We are invited
to hold the space of
compassion during loss,
grace in disorientation,
kindness in grief.

If we yield to the process of *waiting in darkness* with the one we are caring for, we too will be filled with wonder and awe as the day comes when light emerges from the chrysalis and we witness the formation of wings, the transformation of a life.

A piece of art, a writing of poetry, a radiant countenance are indications to me that a person has emerged from this darkness and is now allowing the sun to fill their wings with the energy they need for the flight ahead. As one who has accompanied many in their darkness, my own heart surges with wonder and gratitude for what we both experience in such moments and can hardly name. To witness wings is to witness hope, and I've had the joy of knowing this hope many times in the beautiful service of souls.

Embracing Inner Solitude

In the work I do in circles through retreats and Soul Care programs, I often use the phrase: *"alone and yet together; together, yet alone."* There's an aspect of this journey where we all must find the courage to enter the dark wood, the dark chrysalis ... *alone.* Even though as a friend of your soul I may accompany you on some level, you must also walk alone. In and down, to the path of your descent, you are the only one to do your inner work. You must have the courage to navigate the inner landscape, to listen to your precious heart, to yield in dissolving your form, to trust and surrender in the midst of loss. Those are things that no one can do for another. There's an inner resolve, a determination that one must grasp to plunge into the darkness that we all have before us. As Gertrud writes: "To withdraw into solitude is a conscious entry into our wounded reality and also into introspection and inner work where dreams, stories, Scripture, prayer, poetry and the message of the inner world are taken in slowly and lovingly.[16]"

There are a million distractions. None of us *have* to do this. Many don't. But it's always an invitation. Wisdom sings to us: "Will you enter the beautiful darkness of formation? The place of hiddenness, disorientation, unknowing?"

Will you enter the beautiful darkness
of formation?
The place of hiddenness, disorientation,
unknowing?

This song continues: "Don't you want to come to the place where you will have to give up everything you've ever known that is your identity?" No wonder we're afraid. What will we have to give up? What will we lose? One friend spoke to me as we contemplated this journey: "I'm afraid of being annihilated." Yes, that fear is in all of us. Our ego is afraid. But what is the treasure we will find? I believe it is here that we find our very lives, our precious souls, and we discover and perhaps cherish for the first time the diamond within. From this place of transformation, a new life begins—of *meaning, integrity, fidelity, and vitality.*

No one can enter the woods for another. I have invited many. Few come. At first, in my excitement of tasting transformation, I tried to coerce people into the woods. "*Come with me! Come and find the*

16   Gertrud Mueller Nelson Here All Dwell Free (New York: Doubleday, 1991) 125.

treasure of your soul with me." I soon realized that this was not my task. It's up to each soul to choose. We always must accompany people wherever they are at. Some are looking at the woods cautiously, and others are deeply in. We're invited to hold a posture of quiet invitation and to keep doing our own inner work of letting our roots down to the wellspring. In this way we can be a healthy tree of solace and comfort for those who enter. We too will be invited "deeper in, deeper in." There is more for us to learn and deeper soil to allow our roots to grow into. Our work is never complete. It's only beginning, and we too can humbly surrender to the formation that Love is calling us to.

Journey of Transformation

Transformation through darkness often leads to expansion. Our culture sees expansion as something to attain or possess; however, inner expansion comes from an opposite energy—losing form, allowing, surrendering, and yielding to a *process.* Expansion that emerges from this process carries a vitality, beauty, truth, and a reality that can only be known as ... resurrection. One may understand the phrase *"I was dead, but now I live"* in an inner way, a way of the soul.

Chapter XVI

Compassionate Witness—Friend of Tears

Tears. Why do we so often apologize for our tears? There seems to be a shame attached with allowing our tears to be experienced and seen by others; however, those who have trudged through the healing journey know that tears do a good work in us, much like the womb creates a space for formation. Tears, when expressed, are alchemical, holy, and they transmit something from the inside to the outside. They are a tangible expression of the confusion, grief, or sadness our heart needs to express.

Holding Back Tears

People hold their tears back for different reasons, and many of these can be unconscious. One of the reasons I've experienced is that they have witnessed tears being used as a tool of emotional manipulation by another. They fear, that by expressing their tears, they will be like the one they have disdained or that they will be misunderstood as emotionally needy and manipulative.

Others hold back because they've numbed themselves from their emotions for years. Allowing tears to emerge is to open a Pandora's box of feeling that they don't feel ready for. Sometimes the person has never had the experience of another being hospitable with their emotional expression. In this case, there's a tremendous fear of rejection or alienation if a strong emotion is allowed. Culturally, we tend not to welcome tears, so there is general embarrassment about crying in front of another. However, the body (knowing the truth of our humanity and carrying the wisdom of how we heal) longs for release from pent-up pain and tears are one of the gifts our bodies has to help us unpack suffering held within.

Tears as Physical Release

We store in our bodies the trauma, pain, and grief we have known. Releasing our tears is a way for the body to feel, acknowledge, and turn toward the suffering. Crying doesn't necessarily mean that we're holding on; it often means we're ready to let go. Tears help us to *feel* in our body what we need to feel. Most people are trying not to feel and would rather stay distracted and disconnected from whatever pain is chasing them.

To stop and allow the tears to emerge is to allow an *integration with our suffering* into wholeness. It's only when we face our pain that we're able to heal. Bottling our tears and pushing down our feelings is like trying to keep a ball under water. Another day or in another way our pain will show up. Maybe it will be through sickness. Maybe it will be through a crisis. Maybe it will be through depression. We aren't designed to push our suffering away. It's human, deeply human, to allow our tears.

Inner Container for Tears

Sometimes the inner container of healing needs to grow before we can allow our tears to flow in safety with ourselves and others. In my experience, as a person deepens in their soul journey, it's as though their capacity, their inner container, becomes larger, and they can "hold" or "be with" stronger emotional experiences without the same sense of overwhelm as they had before. The process of becoming deeply rooted within helps them to be a loving presence to their own dear hearts especially when the healing tears flow. It can feel like an irony that as a person is feeling stronger and more rooted that their submerged pain emerges in a significant way, but it's normal. The pain was waiting until there was a large enough container for it to be held in love. It can feel for them like they're going backwards in their soul journey, but the truth is they're right on track. The walk is a slow walk as we deepen our roots and allow our full selves to emerge, pain and all.

Long Journey of Tears

For a period of three years, I cried every day. I entered a season of tears that just didn't seem to stop. I wondered if my tears would ever end. I felt embarrassed and ashamed of all those tears, but when they finally eased, I realized their sacredness. Those tears acknowledged the depths of suffering and pain. Those tears told the story of what happened. Those tears kept me close to what I needed to feel and process. As Spiritual Directors, we may encounter people who will enter a journey of tears. Sometimes it's for one session, but for others, it may be a long season of tears. It may seem endless. It may seem tiresome. It may seem difficult. But we are invited to be with these tears.

Compassionate Witness

As Spiritual Directors, our posture toward tears is one of *compassionate witness*, to be present and to acknowledge the suffering of another. I'm reminded of visiting the Killing Fields in Cambodia, a site where more than a million people were tortured and killed from 1975 to 1979. In 2007, I walked through the fields and buildings where people had suffered horrendously and been murdered. Old shards of bones were still in the earth and visible to the eye. Piles of skulls were placed in a monument. Torture chambers in lonely, dark hallways lingered with eerie quiet. Even though those who had suffered there were now passed, I felt a stirring to speak to those souls and say, *"I witness you now."* As I walked, I wept. *"I witness your suffering. Even though you were unseen at the time, I witness you now."*

This is often the energy I hold with those letting me know of their suffering, their tears. They felt alone, invisible, forgotten in the abuse, grief, and trauma they experienced. We walk through the empty rooms and hallways of their life and cry together, acknowledging, *"We witness you now. We witness you now."* It's powerful to be witnessed. It's one human saying to another through our posture of attentiveness that they matter, they count, they are significant, even if they were so alone when the suffering happened. We can witness together now and cry holy tears of acknowledgement.

No Need for Pity

This posture of compassionate witness is not a pitying posture. One of the things I learned from both Joy and Doreen is that they never felt sorry for me. In those early years with Joy, I cried with my pain in every session, and I never felt her bend toward pity. What she did was *hold space for my suffering*, and this was a very different energy. She didn't coddle me or get mad on my behalf. She simply entered into my suffering with me by witnessing me. Then, as I was ready, she invited me to open my heart to Love's invitation *in the midst* of my suffering. In the end, this was empowering. My child-self wanted to be pitied, but that would have kept me in an infantile state. Joy's ability to offer loving presence in the midst of suffering allowed my heart to heal in being witnessed and to choose to respond to Love's invitation.

When we're tempted to pity another, we must look at our own hearts. What need are we trying to meet in ourselves by pitying the one we're listening to? What wound are we attempting to fix in the other that is not our responsibility? It can be painful to be present to another person's pain. We may feel trauma as we witness their trauma. We may be horrified at the suffering of another. It may rip our hearts open.

Sometimes my heart has simply broken on behalf of another, and my own tears well up as I hold the posture of compassionate witness. Yet I cannot take their suffering away. I cannot fix their wounds. This is not my work, even though I may want to heal and satiate the longing for wholeness. It is paramount in moments like these that I become aware of the Living Presence in the room with us. This Living, Loving Presence attends to all our hidden places of suffering, entering our grief alongside us. In moments like these, we are invited to pause, to breathe, to become aware of Love with us in our suffering. There are no words here, only presence. And this presence is enough.

> *In moments like these,*
> *we are invited to pause,*
> *to breathe,*
> *to become aware of Love with us in our suffering.*
> *There are no words here,*
> *only presence.*
> *And this presence is enough.*

Tears from our Losses

Other times in my life tears have come with the sudden loss of a loved one or prolonged grief regarding something I can't fix. I know there is no one who can remedy a death or fix something that has been broken, but there's a release in my body when the tears can come as a way of acknowledging the impact of loss. Loss carries impact. It's like a tree losing a branch. Perhaps it's even a healthy loss, a necessary loss. But it is still loss. And tears may be a way of acknowledging the impact of that loss. Years after my divorce, I had a session with Doreen in which the grief of past loss emerged and tears of the impact of this loss welled up. Doreen moved to sit beside me and opened her arms to me. "You can cry," she said. And I did until it passed.

Loss comes in all sorts of forms: death, divorce, illness, change of vocation, loss of singleness, loss of marriage, loss of freedom, loss of family. Loss is truly about *change—letting go of the way we have known things to be.* In some ways, loss invites us into the darkness of the chrysalis. We return to the darkness of not knowing and dissolve the form we have known into cellular mush. And loss is one of the great constants in our lives. It is also one of the reasons people come for Spiritual Direction. Loss, the disorientation of life as we have known it, can bring us to our knees and open our hearts in a way we have never faced before.

Sally

Sally came for her appointment but let me know she didn't even know what to talk about. As is often the case when this happens, I invited us to be still and breathe together. Then she told me that she had been having pain in her jaw and it was really bothering her. I asked her to describe her discomfort to me, and she said it was across her entire face. Having no medical training, I had no idea what was going on, but I listened. And then I listened some more. I asked her if this pain had come before. Sally began to tell me about when it first had happened in her life, over twenty years earlier when her son had died.

As she began to share about her son's unexpected passing all those years ago, we both recognized that her body was responding to a grief she wasn't connecting with consciously, so we turned to what her body was telling her now. What grief was emerging that she was cognitively unaware of? The tears came as she connected with her body in this way, recognizing that there was a return of grief for the precious son who had died. There was nothing really to talk about, but there was an invitation to be present to a grief and to recognize the need for tears and release.

Molly's Story—Permission for Tears

In Soul Care circles, we talk about fidelity to our souls, the inner commitment to listen and to honour the truth of ourselves, living from our deepest integrity. Molly shared with me her journey of tears and how it connected with fidelity to her soul. These are her words:

I can't remember the exact date it happened, but at work I was hurt (emotionally), and in my mind, heart, and soul I vowed that I would not cry. In the moments that followed I felt a deep sense of betrayal to myself, deeper than I have felt in this journey so far. It was like I finally really understood what fidelity to my soul truly meant to me. It was a vow that I haven't uttered in months, and it hurt more than the words spoken. I ended up in the bathroom and allowed myself to cry a little ... but the impact has stayed with me. I have begun to process it a bit more, and the other night I wrote this poem, or rather this poem exploded out of my heart and onto the paper.

The beauty of this is that writing poetry, and possibly other forms of writing (not sure what that means), is beginning to bloom in me. I have always enjoyed writing but never allowed myself to explore it, thinking I wasn't good enough, but it's not really about that anymore. So writing is becoming a place of growth yet a place of real vulnerability for me.

"I will not cry."
The words that now kill my heart
The words that are lies to my soul
The words that do NOT make me strong in my weak moments
The words that are now a LIE

I will cry
TRUTH to myself
STRENGTH when I feel weak
I will cry

FREEDOM to my pain
RELEASE to be my true self

"NOT" is no longer allowed
"SHAME" no longer will have a voice
I will allow the beauty of my rain to fall down my cheeks
I will cry

Friend of Tears

As we listen to others, we may meet people in their time of greatest vulnerability. We are invited to be a compassionate witness and a friend of tears. As we hold the posture of compassionate witness, we do so rooted and grounded in Love. This allows for the expression of necessary grief and also lays the ground for healing for the soul.

I see Psalm 23 as a beautiful model for living and offering this kind of presence. The beginning of the psalm invites us to rest, to lie down. We are invited to be weak, to be fragile, to be still. It's in this posture of rest that our souls are restored and renewed. Our hearts are healed through beauty and awareness that we are not alone. "Even though I walk through the valley of the shadow ... you are with me" (Psalm 23:4). We learn that we are accompanied in our most difficult times. We are invited to receive at the table in the midst of challenge. The Table is another symbol of fellowship, communion, and nurture. Finally, the journey of Psalm 23 brings us to blessing. We are anointed with oil and blessed for the journey.

Chapter XVII

Living out of the Gaze of Love

What does it mean to live out of the gaze of Love? This is a grace I have learned to know, and it has become an anchor in my life, a way to come home, a way to stay oriented to the truth of my being. Living out of the gaze of Love is an inner reality that guides my life as a pilgrim on the journey and as a Spiritual Director for other soul pilgrims. The only way I can describe this posture and reality to you is by telling you a story.

A Story of Receiving the Gaze of Love

It was 2006. I had been on this soul journey for seven years, and so much had transpired. I was freer in many ways and had begun to write music for the first time in years and share my creativity with the community I was a part of. I was in the process of recording the first album of my life. It was incredibly exciting for me after so much turmoil and pain, but one day an old wound reared its head up again. I felt like I was back where I had started, and I felt sorry for myself. Out of sorts and anxious, I reached out to a friend for support. This person responded with these words: "Cathy, rest." Rest? *Rest?* This response to my request for help made me feel very angry. *How dare you tell me to rest when I am struggling! How dare you tell me to rest when I need support!*

As much as I was enraged with these words, they tugged at me. I had done enough soul work by then to know there was a ring of truth in them that was calling me to pay attention. I decided to respond by actually lying down on my bed to enter rest and stillness in the midst of my great frustration. What I experienced next was perhaps a vision, or perhaps I fell asleep and had a dream. I simply don't know. But I can tell you what my eyes beheld, what my ears heard, and how it changed the course of my life.

I saw myself as a baby bird at the top of a large tree in a huge forest with hundreds of other trees. This baby bird was squawking and flapping her wings wildly. She was yelling, "MAMA! MAMA! WHERE ARE YOU?" There were no other creatures in the forest. She was alone and desperate. In the quiet of the wood, she squawked and flapped her wings. Suddenly, over the canopy of trees, a great mother bird sailed through the sky. She swooped and soared and came right to the freaking-out baby bird—me. She planted herself on the side of the nest and put one wing on my right cheek and the other wing on my left. Then she said these words, which ring in my ears to this day: "Look at me. Look at me! Look at me ... until you become ... the reflection of me."

As I looked at Mama Bird's eyes, they captivated me. I felt the energy of my own eyes, wild with panic and fear. I realized the eyes I was now looking at held a completely different reality. At the centre of her eyes was the utmost calm. They were serene, like a completely peaceful, still tranquil lake. On the outer rims of her eyes was a sense of laughter and playfulness, lightness and joy. These eyes held an invitation to look. To look and look and look. I realized these eyes had so much to teach me. These eyes were not afraid. These eyes were not frantic. These eyes were full of depth and love. They held a serenity, a tranquility with a framework of laughter. They held compassion, truth-telling, and fearlessness. They held knowing, seeing, and total acceptance. These eyes *knew* something that I didn't know... and I dedicated myself to this gaze.

"Look at me.
Look at me!
Look at me...
until you become...
the reflection of me."

It is in entering this gaze of Love that I learned so much. It taught me that it was my work to look and receive, that in truly looking and soaking in what Love was releasing toward me, I would be changed. I didn't know it at the time, but that is what happened. As Mama Bird said, if I looked, I would become the reflection of this gaze. My work was to look.

It was years later when I found myself at a retreat centre and a couple bumped into me in a hallway. They were lost and didn't know how to find their way. I began to show them around and we ended up having a lovely conversation. As we prepared to say goodbye, the husband turned to me and said, "There's something about your eyes; they're calm and yet full of laughter. What is it about you?" Stunned to hear these words, as I had never spoken of my Mama Bird experience, I went to my room and lay on the bed and wept. Could it be that a small degree of reflection was living in me? Could it be that I was reflecting this gaze of Love? *What grace! What wonder!* What a miracle of transformation in my life.

Invitation to Look at Love

We are invited to "look" at Love loving us. This posture of receptivity isn't passive but open and vulnerable. It is child-like and tender. And if we allow it, it is the place of true transformation. We live out of the gaze of *wherever we put our attention*. What is our gaze upon? Where is our focus? In psychology, we learn about the impact of "mirroring." Infants especially are caught up in gazing at their primary caregivers. What do those faces tell the infant? We mirror back the gaze we receive. Many of us have not known healthy mirroring, and we reflect what we see looking at us: more fear, more pain, more anxiety, more judgement.

We are invited to live out of the Gaze of Love. There are many distractions every single day that pull us away from the Gaze of Love. We get hooked into situations, problems, worry, fear. Our gaze becomes fixed on a myriad of things that pull us down into despair and anxiety. When I recognize that I am "off," I know my gaze has been distracted. Even in the midst of very difficult events, I have learned to re-focus my inner energy on Love, and Love's gaze has guided an inner knowing of a goodness, a beauty, a joy that undergirds all things. This gaze has guided me through many, many situations where I didn't know what to do. We are invited to hold a posture of this gaze within. This requires time to *pause*. STOP! REST! We must have time to fully stop everything. We must rest and look. We must rest and receive. We must reorient our gaze and know the truth of Love.

We must rest and look.
We must rest and receive.
We must reorient and know the truth of Love.

Love's energy is a powerful, quiet energy that is radiant with joy and laughter. Love's energy is dynamic, inviting, without fear, and creative. Love's energy is *generative* and wild for truth. This is the energy we are meant to know and to live out of. This is the energy that heals, calms, soothes, teaches, and transforms. We don't *do* this work, but we *receive* it and then carry the fruit of it in our lives, which spills over into others.

A Lifestyle of Looking, Receiving the Gaze
My life has been blessed with mystical moments that I know are not everyone's experience. I don't expect everyone else to have a Mama Bird story; however, I believe that the essence or heart of that experience

is available to us all in countless measures. Jesus taught us to look at the lilies. What might they teach us? They don't toil or spin. Look at the birds. They are singing. Look at the smile of a child. Look at the curve of the moon. *Look. Look. Look.* Perhaps the Gaze of Love will meet you through the ordinary elements around you in unexpected ways and in unexpected moments. When you meet this gaze, you'll be invited to learn and to expand as Love fills you. You will taste wonder. You will taste beauty. You will taste laughter. This gaze will fill you and give you grace to be a container in the midst of suffering. This Gaze of Love, filling us, undergirds all suffering.

> *This gaze of Love,*
> *filling us,*
> *undergirds all suffering.*

There is so much mystery in life and so much we cannot understand about suffering; however, we can know the Presence of Love, the Gaze of Love *in the midst* of suffering, even as I did in that simple way on my bed. We can hold the depths of this gaze as we are present to the suffering of others. Love invited me to *look* in the midst of my confusion and allow Love's energy to change my orientation, my response. As Spiritual Directors, we are invited to receive this gaze to sustain us as we listen to others. We are invited to let this gaze heal us and transform us. And finally, we are meant to become bearers of this gaze, allowing the Gaze of Love to flow through us as we love those around us.

Learning from the Life of Christ

This gaze of Love is so beautifully reflected in the life of Jesus to many who gathered around Him. As I conversed with Doreen, she shared these words with me: "We look to Jesus when we want to know the human reality of what God looks like and lived in and among us. We always lean into the way Jesus was: how he looked at people, how he touched people, listened to people, stood with people. We see who he drew into healing and who he attracted. We let *ourselves* be seen in the context of his reality, and then *we become what we have lived.* We become *how we have been looked at.* This is not an intellectual exercise—it's an *embodiment.* We learn from the inside what it is to be beloved, and from this place, we become part of the emerging presence of God in the world. This leads us to be responsive rather than reactive as we engage with life. This has been my practice: a contemplative reality, a way of life."

Looking Wherever You Are

Living lives that carry awareness of stillness, attentiveness, and presence awakens us to the Gaze of Love. Sometimes we think that contemplation only comes when we are utterly alone and silent, but contemplation is a *way of the heart.* Gazing is an act of the soul. Looking and noticing can be known in every single moment if we bring our attention to it. If you are a parent of young children and have a busy life, you can be attentive to the moments that are around you. You can become aware of the softness of a child's cheek, the beauty of the sunset as you drive to soccer practice, the smell of soup as you pour it for your family. If you live alone, you can become aware of the sounds of silence, the rhythms of nature around you, the sacredness of time.

We all can learn to look no matter who or where we are. Find beauty. Look at what you see. Look deeply at what you see. Let it look back at you. Let it speak to you. Let your heart receive. It is here that you will know transformation.

Find beauty.
Look at what you see.
Look deeply at what you see.
Let it look back at you.
Let it speak to you.
Let your heart receive.
It is here that you will know transformation.

After journeying in Spiritual Direction for eighteen months, Ruth left our final session with these words: "I came as broken glass. But you saw me. You looked in my eyes. And now I am stained glass, beautiful and melded together." Years later she added these words: "You are forever held in my heart; you gently helped me feel again. You taught me the importance of acknowledging my wounded soul, allowing healing and wholeness into my spirit."

"I came as broken glass.
But you saw me.
You looked in my eyes.
And now I am stained glass,
beautiful and melded together."

Chapter XVIII

Mother Wounds/Father Wounds

As Denise began to describe her dilemma about the decision before her, and her heart's desire to listen and discern how she was being guided, she released some unexpected frustration. "Well, why even listen? Why pray? God isn't really interested in the details of my life anyway." I started really paying attention. *Hmmm. God isn't interested? What else is this God like?* I invited Denise to describe her "God" to me.

"Well, He's absent, and when I try to pray, I don't feel heard or seen. It's just easier if I get things done on my own."

The energy of her statements filled the room. I invited us to enter silence for a few moments as my heart pondered her words. First, God was male. Second, God was absent. Third, God was unreliable. The silence brought me awareness of a deep sadness and loneliness underneath these words. An ache. "Denise, I'm wondering if you've had these feelings in any other situation in your life?"

A slow dawn of awareness came over Denise's face. "Oh my gosh. This is about my father."

Our Projections from Unhealed Places Within

Whatever is unhealed in us gets projected onto others and even onto the Divine Presence. Suddenly, "God" is all sorts of things belonging to our imagination and past wounds. When we listen to someone in Spiritual Direction, we're invited to hear the words they are saying and the words they are not saying. The invitation is always to bring us into greater alignment with Love, unity with Presence, awareness of our Source. Anything that blocks us from Love or covers over the truth of this Love is something to become aware of. Just becoming *aware* of a projection can change our attitude, our process of discernment.

As Denise became aware of this father projection regarding a process of decision making, she could reorient herself to what she had known to be true in her own life with the Divine Presence. She *was* seen. She *was* known. She *was* loved. She *was* accompanied. Inner peace returned, and a sense of calm entered our session again. However, there was now awareness of a shadow to turn toward: the shadow of a painful relationship with her father that wasn't healed or integrated in her life, which caused her to throw projections around in an unconscious way.

Awareness Brings Invitation

With *every* awareness comes an *invitation*. Many people sigh and get overwhelmed when a shadow emerges. It can feel embarrassing and shameful to see an aspect of ourselves that isn't whole and beautiful. However, if we are dedicated to soul work, it is a *gift* to see another shadow, for it's another opportunity to align in a greater way with Love, a way to realize one's own blindness, and an opportunity to see more clearly. This is the hard work of turning toward our pain and allowing it to teach us about ourselves, about the past, and about Love's invitation.

The Enneagram, a typology of nine personality types, is a tool in self-understanding. This resource is very helpful in bringing aware-ness to some of the core areas of pain that many of us hold, such as not feeling seen, heard, acknowledged, valued, etc. Usually, there is a younger part of us that has formed a belief from what we've experienced in the past, and we feel it to be true. When we experience a hint of that similar feeling through a current relationship or situation, it validates this inner core belief that began so long ago. The core beliefs that can form from our primal areas of pain are: I am invisible. I am not valuable. I am not worthy, etc. We are largely unconscious of these inner beliefs, as they began at a very young age. But they affect everything we are and do, as well as our inner spiritual lives, in tremendous ways.

First Beliefs Arise from our Primary Caregivers

Our first beliefs about ourselves and about the way of love come from our primary caregivers, most often our mother and father.

What is your first instinct regarding your mother?
Did you feel safe, nurtured, listened to, seen?
Did you feel protected, cared for, provided for, acknowledged?

What is your first instinct regarding your father?
Did you feel welcomed, celebrated, honoured?
Did you experience blessing, guidance, and affirmation?

What do these words do for you?
Do they create a longing in you?
Do they create an ache?

Do they remind you of good memories you can be grateful for?
Do they remind you of what you received or what you lacked?

Notice.
Pay attention.

Continued Healing for Us All

The vast majority of us have father and mother wounds. What those wounds might be are unique to each of our lives. Our work is to become aware of how we might be projecting the stories of our past onto others and into our spiritual life. As Spiritual Directors, we're invited to continue to heal the areas of mother and father wounds within and to keep healing so that we can offer spaces of healing for others in a generous manner. Perhaps some of this healing will continue for the rest of our lives, but it is so worth every ounce of energy we put into it. Every healing brings a greater degree of freedom. Freedom in our relationships is freedom to respond to things as they actually are instead of through the filters from the past. The more we can be fully present, the more we carry a loving presence that is pure. This is our work and the way of living we invite others into.

Our Family History

Many of the mother/father wounds we deal with come from a long line of patterns. In my own family tree, there are at least four generations of orphans. I wasn't conscious of this reality in my family but lived with an inner orphan energy and, in fact, married an orphan at the age of nineteen. When I began to study my family history and all the stories that I knew and didn't know, I realized how I was continuing a story through my beliefs about myself that were deeply unconscious yet so powerful. I began a journey of re-parenting myself through receiving the grace of Love. Love began to heal me in the places where I had both mother and father wounds. My parents did the best they could, but there were large gaps in what they were able to provide, as they were unaware of what was unfinished in them and being passed down through them over many generations.

The work of contemplation, slowing down, paying attention, stillness, and prayer led to a growing awareness of my inner wounds. This awareness wasn't easy to acknowledge, but each awareness held an invitation to turn toward the pain and the shadow and allow a greater alignment with Love, with the truth of my being. Some of this work was explored with Spiritual Direction, some on my own, and some with a Jungian analyst as we worked with my dreams for a period of two and a half years. It was all a journey of awareness, invitation, and healing. The more I understood of these patterns with mother/father wounds, the more I could open up to the process of healing. Healing brought increased freedom within. Freedom within brought greater release of creativity, joy, vitality, and compassion for self and others.

> *Freedom in our relationships*
> *is freedom to respond to things as they actually are*
> *instead of through the filters from the past.*

Sometimes I will ask a directee to find out more about their family system, the relationships of their mothers and grandmothers, fathers and grandfathers. We aren't solo units here on earth. We're part of a tapestry of relationships, and those relationships impact how we respond to our own lives and all those around us. The more we can become aware of the dynamics of the tapestry we're in, the more we can awaken to healing and integration in our own lives.

Healing of Divine Father/Mother

Although my marriage came to an end after twenty-four years, I learned so much through that relationship. I had been projecting some of my deep mother/father needs onto my husband. There was a lot of parenting that I needed in my life that I was looking for in others. The orphan in me was yearning for things another person simply couldn't fulfill. I had to learn to receive this from Divine Love. Over time, I learned the magnificent energy of Divine Mother. She is wild, fierce, generative, and tender. I learned the wondrous energy of Divine Father. He is full of blessing, runs toward and delights in me. My cup has been filled. My cup runs over. Through receiving over and over, I have known transformation. I am now able to open my arms wide and allow others to come in. My heart says: *Come and know the embrace of Love. Come and feel the delight of Love! Come and rest in the nurture of Love.*

Wholeness Is Like a Tree

I believe the beauty and wholeness of life is like a tree. I need to go down to my roots and receive, over and over, this Divine Love. It fills me, reminds me of what is true, and restores my soul. As I receive, I'm able to extend my branches into the world without fear and with a sense of abundance and rest. We *are* able to heal from very deep wounds. We *are* able to be restored from places of lack. We *are* able to know unconditional love and acceptance. We *are* able to feel parented and to learn to stand as adults and not as children in the world. I believe we are meant to hold an energy of child-likeness as we continue to receive what we need. But we are meant to *grow up* and let go of being childish. We are meant to move as beings who are whole. This is our inheritance. It's there for us to receive.

> *Come and know the embrace of Love.*
> *Come and feel the delight of Love!*
> *Come and rest in the nurture of Love.*

In Spiritual Direction, many will come to us looking for father/ mother wounds to be met. It's real and a natural thing to do. But we must be aware of this projection and hold it with grace when it shows up. We personally can't meet that inner need of the father/mother, but we can hold grace for the healing of that need. Our work is to be rooted ourselves in knowing the unconditional Love that is within and all around. We can hold the energy of this healing Love and allow Love to guide our sessions through deep listening and attentiveness to grace.

Healing of these inner wounds may take years and a dedication to awareness and facing pain. Much patience is required for the one healing and the one listening. However, I believe in the healing of Love. It is a mystery and not a process we can control in ourselves or another. It's not a surgery that we understand fully how to conduct. Transformation is a grace that we open to and allow. It is again the place of receiving. And when transformation occurs in our lives, we look with wonder and say, "Surely Love was in this place."

Transformation is a grace
that we open to and allow.
It is again the place of receiving.
And when transformation occurs in our lives,
we look with wonder and say,
"Surely Love was in this place."

Chapter XIX

Letting it All Go—The Art of Nothingness

There is a Tibetan Buddhist tradition of creating sand art mandalas as prayer. This is an elaborate task by a team of Buddhist monks using coloured sand and stones that can take up to several weeks. These mandalas are incredible works of art, full of detail and intricate beauty. After the mandala is complete and the prayer rituals are done, the sand is collected in silk and taken to a body of water, usually a river, and released into it.

Ritual of Letting Go

When I first saw pictures of this ritual and heard the story of how it was carried out, I was captivated. It held so much symbolic meaning for me. This ritual became a metaphor for the soul work I have devoted my life to. Facilitating a Soul Care retreat, seeing someone for a Spiritual Direction hour, preparing an evening of sung prayers all can be a great devotion of my time, creativity, and energy. I may pour myself into the minute details of a person's life, a song, a meditation experience. I may devote a great deal of intensity to seeing something beautiful happen either in an individual or a group. And when this moment is complete, it's my job to wrap it up in silk and bring it to the river and let it go.

Letting the beauty of our work go is so important. We're not to hang on, even when it's good. We're to entrust it to the river, to the flow of Love, to wherever it needs to go. It is not ours. It doesn't belong to us. We were gifted with a moment of grace with a person, a group, a situation. But this moment or experience, time of wonder and beauty, doesn't increase our value or our identity. It's a gift we all tasted ... and we need to entrust it back from where it came.

Anita's Story

Anita had a rough story. Her father had been killed when she was eleven years old, and she had been a witness to his murder. There was deep trauma in her body, and as a grown woman, she was facing the pain of this through our times together in Spiritual Direction. In one session, her grief emerged in a way that was deep and intense. I sat across from her, holding space for her tears and sorrow. As her tears emerged in even more intensity, I offered to sit beside her if she wished. She let me know that was okay, so I moved and sat beside her. A lullaby welled up in my heart, and I began to hum and sing for her as she wept. We entered holy ground as we waded through the raw energy of the past in stillness and humming. In time, it was complete. There was a sense of it being done. She turned to me in gratitude before she left. There were no words, only understanding. After she was gone, I sat in silence a while longer. The time had impacted me, and I needed to let it go. I needed to wrap it up in silk and place it in the river of Love. It was now in Love's hands. Not knowing how this would change her life or if we would ever speak of it again, I let go.

Art of Nothingness

We need to be okay with the art of nothingness, our hands remaining open, not gripping or clinging to the good or the bad of our lives. We live with open hands, not attaching ourselves to outcome or proof of the gift in the moment.

We live with open hands,
not attaching ourselves to outcome
or proof of the gift in the moment.

We let it go. We let it go. *We let it go.* The art of nothingness allows us to continue to be present to the moment that is now. Hanging on keeps locked-in something that happened. Whether good or bad, it's easy to stay and cling. To live with letting it all go means that we can continue to receive what is actually unfolding in that very moment. We're able to stay present, grounded, rooted, here. This is the art of nothingness. Non-attachment.

When our work is so deep and involves many, many details of another's life, we can become entrenched or overburdened. We can become bent-over, consumed, and our posture can knock us over and cause burnout, depression, and anxiety. We are invited to let the details go, over and over and over, into the river of Love. The blessings and the challenges, all back in the river. This allows us freedom, lightness of heart, and an ability to carry on.

Empty Hands ... Ready Hands

Years later, I overheard Anita in a group share of this experience and how much it had meant to her. It moved me deeply to know that the gift from that moment had impacted her life and brought a sense of healing to a very raw place. It was a grace to know that—not a right, but a precious little kiss from Love, a little thank-you my heart quietly received. Most of the work, however, is one of not knowing the outcome. I've recognized that this is actually a great gift. It frees me to *not know*, to not be attached to any outcome. What has occurred is between that person and Love ... it is no longer in my hands. I have wrapped it in silk and let it go. My hands become empty but ready to once again move with Love's invitation.

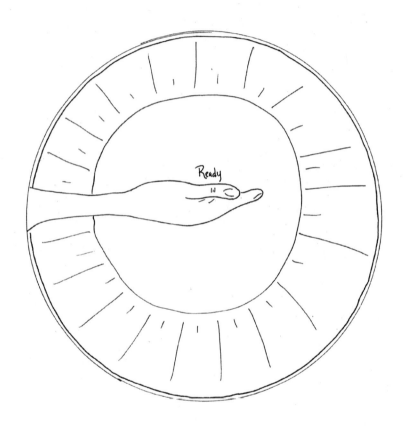

Chapter XX

Healing Practices for Use in Spiritual Direction

There are different modalities of Spiritual Direction, different forms and practices. Spiritual Direction comes from a long line of history in many of the indigenous/spiritual/religious traditions, in which one has a mentor, a wise elder, an *anam cara* (meaning *soul friend* in Gaelic), a confessor. Most of the great mystics from various spiritual traditions had another soul with whom they could share their inner spiritual journey. These relationships were formative and offered guidance and instruction. Some offered healing practices as well. The healing practices of Spiritual Direction came to me in an indirect manner. No one said they were offering healing. In fact, there was never any mention of healing at all that I can remember. But I do remember being healed. Here are some practices I have known healing through and now offer to others.

Untangling the Knots

There is an icon of Mary, the Mother of Jesus, as the Undoer of Knots. Pope Francis encountered this icon in a time of personal distress while studying in Germany in the 1980s, and it became an image that helped to heal and restore his soul. After I heard this story, I began to think about my own inner knots and how places inside of me felt like tangles or knotted jewelry. The tangled strands of various necklaces can be hard to undo. In the past when I've tried to untangle jewellery by pulling or yanking, the knot becomes more entrenched. It requires great patience, some jewellery tools, and gentle hands to pull apart what has become knotted together. This metaphor of the untangling of knots became symbolic for me in my own life and as I began to sit with the lives of others.

Exercise of Untangling the Knots

I created an exercise called "Untangling the Knots" that has helped me and many others to explore our inner landscape in a healing way. First of all, I draw a small circle at the centre of a blank page. In that circle, I identify and name a knot that is tangled within. This may be a conflict with another person, a place of discernment, a fear, an old memory, etc. It can be anything at all that feels tangled. Usually there's a real physical sensation of tightness in the body around inner issues that are left unresolved. Bringing a name to our knot helps us to begin.

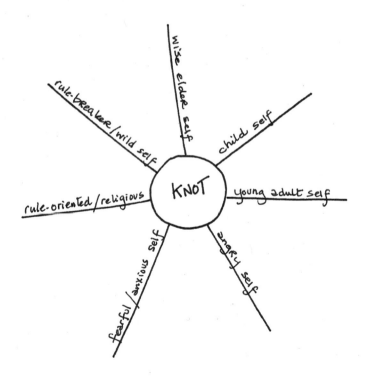

Secondly, I draw seven spokes coming out of this inner circle. These seven spokes become places to write seven archetypes that we all share. Other archetypes may be added, but I find these are common to many and can open a gateway of understanding and release. The first archetype is the young child. I write "child" on the first spoke coming out of the wheel and then proceed to feel and write what my inner child wants to say regarding the issue at the centre. I allow my inner child to speak without editing her. What so often happens with our inner dialogue is that my child self has something to say, something to express, but another part of me, perhaps my rule-oriented self, is condescending toward that child part of me and shuts down what needs to be explored. This is a practice in letting go of self-editing.

The seven archetypes I often invite people to explore are: Child, Young Adult, Angry, Anxious/Fearful, Wild/Rule-breaker, Religious/ Do-Gooder, Wise Elder. I invite them to first of all feel and then write from these various "voices of self." There is often much awareness that comes with the writing. Awareness brings beliefs or feelings from our shadows into light, into consciousness. When we see and understand the various voices within, we can become more conscious of our inner struggle.

After people write from the various archetypes, I invite them to draw a big circle around it all and write the word "LOVE." What if they knew that Love was holding it all? What is Love's response to all the archetypes of self? This becomes a place of inner reflection and listening, a place where the conscious connects with the messages of the unconscious. What do I become aware of? What do I notice? What wisdom emerges?

Robert A Johnson writes "The purpose of learning to work with the unconscious is not just to resolve our conflicts or deal with our neuroses. We find there a deep source of renewal, growth, strength, and wisdom. We connect with the source of our evolving character; we cooperate with the process whereby we bring the total self together; we learn to tap that rich lode of energy and intelligence that waits within."[17]

Stories and Archetypes for Exploration

Entering stories is a way to heal our souls, as stories carry archetypes of images that we all have within. In Jungian psychology there is an invitation to integrate our various archetypes in myths and legends for healing. Any story can open the door of understanding and inner work. Some myths and legends that I have found helpful to explore are: The Handless Maiden, Bluebeard, Manawee, Cinderella, Fisher King, and Alice in Wonderland. As Gertrud Mueller Nelson says: "Fairy tales often begin on the surface: they make some ordinary comment on what is going on in the ordinary, surface world. Then, suddenly, the surface gives way and we are plunged down the well into the inner world."[18] Having time to explore an old story can help us see ourselves in the story we are living. How do we resonate with these characters? What might their challenges speak to our own journey?

Writing our own stories through the lens of a fairy tale or myth can be a way to see our lives through images and metaphors. Entering the imagination with our own life stories in a new way can help integrate the healing in our lives.

Engaging in a Gospel Story

An Ignatian form of prayer involves entering a Gospel story with our imaginations. This form of prayer developed with St. Ignatius as he spent many weeks in convalescence due to an injury from his military experience as a knight in 1521.[19] He began to study the Gospel stories and enter them in his imagination. As he did, he became aware of an

---

17   Robert A. Johnson, Inner Work (New York: HarperCollins, 1989), 9.
18   Gertrud Mueller Nelson Here All Dwell Free (New York: Doubleday, 1991), 4.
19   Eric Jensen, SJ, Ignatius Loyola and You (Toronto: Novalis 2018), 43.

inner form of prayer that brought healing and transformation to his life. This time of convalescence became the foundation of the pathway of the Jesuits, the Ignatian arm of the Catholic Church. The invitation with this form of prayer is to read the story over a few times and then imagine that one is part of the story. We can "see" the scene and, in a sense, take part in the story in a fresh way. By engaging his imagination with the story, St. Ignatius found that the stories began to live within him and bring transformation into his life.

The first time I engaged with a Gospel story this way was in 1998 during my first Silent Retreat. Over a three-day period, I saw a Spiritual Director every day. She invited me into a practice, an old Ignatian practice of using my imagination in prayer. She told me to go off and find a place of solitude on the property and spend an hour focused on a story from the Gospels and imagine myself at the scene. I was to read the story, allow it to fill my imagination, and then interact with what I saw. One of the stories she invited me to ponder was the story of the baptism of Christ. This was a new way of prayer, and at first it felt like work. But as I didn't have anything else to do, I opened myself up to this new experience. I read the story. I read it again. And then I allowed myself to imagine the scene and be there.

Upon entering this retreat, I was still in a state of crisis and new in my journey. I was still feeling the darkness of not knowing and the confusion of loneliness. Joy was the only one at that time who knew the depths of my pain. I felt a great degree of aloneness and, much like Denise's story years later, I wasn't even sure that "God" was aware of all my prayers for help. As I imagined the Gospel story, I was standing in the water beside Jesus and looking out at all the people. I had a strange sensation that I knew them. and that wasn't what I was expecting. I had a sense of my grandparents and others from my past encircling me in those waters. And then, to my utter shock, came a voice I hadn't heard for ten years. A friend from my youth who had passed away on a mountain accident had a distinct voice, an incredibly low and rich-timbered voice. He was a beautiful soul and we had known each other for a number of years before he tragically died. This voice came into that scene and spoke these words: "Cathy, we have heard all of your prayers."

As I sat alone in that sacred space, I wept. I wept and wept and wept. This experience blew away quite a few of my beliefs, and I didn't know what to do with it at the time. I didn't speak of it for a decade, but I often reflected on the scripture about a "cloud of witnesses." *Could it be that I had experienced that cloud? Could it be that my prayers were heard not only by the Divine Presence, but by those who loved me and encircled me? Could it be that I wasn't alone after all? Could it be that there was so much more going on that I would ever know? Could it be that my life was part of a great mystery, and that even though I couldn't see this reality, I could be blessed by the accompaniment of love?* More questions than answers, but the essence of this experience was that *my heart tasted a healing,* a healing of being seen in my aloneness. A healing of being acknowledged in my pain. A healing of being accompanied in my dark night. A healing of kindness in my suffering. This was a very unusual experience for me at that time, but it brought tremendous solace to my heart.

Bringing a Story into Spiritual Direction

There are moments in Spiritual Direction when it seems like an opportunity to offer a directee an invitation to enter a story in their imagination. Sometimes a story will come to mind as they share their story. This is always an invitation. There is the possibility that the directee can do this on their own privately; however, sometimes it has been a gift to pause a session in silence and allow this form of prayer to enter our conversation. I invite the directee to notice what they see and what they become aware of. My work then is to just hold space to be incredibly silent, allowing Love to bring the images to their mind that they need. What has unfolded in this moment has broken my heart open to the work of Love. I fall in love with how Love loves. Images I never could have thought of or created are brought to that person in ways that are healing for them.

Gospel Stories and Archetypes

Some of my favourite Gospel stories in Spiritual Direction are: Peter in the Storm, Jairus's Daughter, the Bent-Over Woman, and the Child on Jesus's Lap. Entering a Gospel story can be another way of exploring archetypes that are universal to us all. This can expand our understanding of an old story as we see it in a new light, in an archetypal way. For example, if we look at the story of the Bent-Over Woman, we could explore the symbolism in this way: Who is the silenced, bent-over woman in me? What part of me has been outcast and stays on the outer part of the circle? What aspect of myself has been rejected? Who have been the religious/institutional accusers? In me? Outside of me? What is the invitation toward truth? What is the invitation toward belonging? How am I renamed? How is my posture invited to rise from being bent-over? Pulling apart a story and exploring the energy that each character contains helps us see aspects of these energies in our own lives. This can be profoundly insightful and healing.

All stories are powerful teachers and help us to understand ourselves and the world we live in. I have experienced many grace-filled moments as I've returned to some of Gospel stories in Spiritual Direction as a pathway for transformation.

Awareness and Questions for Discernment with Inner Work

I was nervous when I began exploring my imagination as a place of healing and prayer. Could it be trusted? Isn't this all a bit subjective? Early on, Joy responded to my questions with wisdom, which has been an anchor to me for all these years. She told me to ask two questions to test if an experience, idea, or situation could be trusted. At the very least, these two questions would help guide the way toward more discernment. And they have. Here are the questions:

1. Is this experience/idea/situation rooted in Love or Fear?
2. What is the fruit of this over time?

Learning to recognize Love energy and Fear energy has taken great attentiveness. Learning to recognize the fruit of something in my life has been a fascinating education. Did this experience, idea, or situation bring peace, joy, love, forgiveness, and trust? I learned first of all to be silent whenever I had a mystical experience or a healing moment that touched me deeply in my imagination, sometimes for a decade. It was time to put the experience in the test tank of fruit- over-time. What does this experience bear in me, in those around me, in my life? What is the root energy of it? Asking these two questions is a wonderful way to offer others a pathway for discernment as they hold a new awareness or a healing moment in their lives.

Years after my own experience, I became aware of others engaging in the imagination for healing through the understanding of Jungian psychology. Robert Johnson, Jungian analyst and author, explains the process of using our imagination for healing in his book, *Inner Work*. It was exciting for me to realize that the imagination is like a new frontier, a place where we can re-work memories and experience living grace. Recent discoveries in quantum physics also affirm the dynamic of our imagination, how engaging healing practices in the mind actually creates the potential to change our cellular nature. *Love changes us.* Love heals us in ways that are real, affecting our very cells. By opening our imagination to Love, we open ourselves to healing places in us that need grace.

Peter... Come... Look at Me...

Joyce's Story

Joyce was afraid ... clearly afraid. I could see her body constrict in tension as she described some of her life circumstances. As we sat in silence after she shared, the story of Peter in the Storm came up in my heart. I invited Joyce to consider this story and asked if she would be open to imagining this story as a form of prayer. Joyce agreed and saw herself in the boat. She saw the fierce waves of the water coming over the boat. In the Gospel story, Jesus is on the shore and invites Peter to walk toward Him. But I just invited Joyce to let her imagination see what it saw and be open to Love's presence in the midst of her storm. She became aware of Love with her in the boat. As this awareness happened, her body released some of its tension and she breathed more deeply. Awareness of Love with her in the storm came to her in a real way in her imagination. We sat in silence as she translated that image to Love *with her now* in the storms of her life. She wasn't alone. She was accompanied. This changed everything.

Exercise—Voices of Accusation

Archetypes in stories carry power for helping us understand on the outside what is happening on the inside. In the Gospel story of what

I call the Stones of Accusation, a woman is accused of adultery and is thrown in front of a crowd who is listening to Jesus teach. The crowd calls out for her to be stoned to death. In that place, Jesus turns to the crowd and says that whoever has not sinned can pick up the first stone. As silence emerges from this request, the crowd disperses one by one.

As I pondered this story, I saw the correlation between the stories I was listening to in Spiritual Direction and the energy of the inner stones of accusation. Janine began telling me of a situation she was struggling with. As she was describing her situation, it was as though another person entered the conversation and accused her of being "too intense," so she edited herself and tried again. This continued, and I could sense her editing her own words and I could feel the inner turmoil of her mind. The archetype of the crowd of accusers rose up in my mind. I became curious what this inner crowd was saying to Janine that caused her to keep changing her words and story.

I asked Janine what was happening to her internally. I let her know that I noticed she was editing herself, and I wondered what was causing that. She shared with me that as she explained her struggle, the old voices she'd always known came pouring in, creating self-doubt and confusion. I then shared with her the story of the woman accused. I suggested that perhaps the stones were like the archetypes of accusation, and that each stone being thrown at her internally was an accusation. I wondered if we could look at these accusations and pull them apart through a simple exercise.

Turning to Love in the Face of Accusations
I invited her to draw a circle at the centre of a piece of paper in her journal and then asked her to put her name at the centre of that circle. Then I invited her to draw another circle around that circle and draw spokes coming out of that second circle. On those spokes I asked her to write down the accusations she was hearing internally. The room became quiet as she wrote down all the interior accusations that had

been filling her as she had been trying to share her story. My heart became very tender as Janine wrote and wrote. There were many inner stones of accusation that she'd been hearing. These archetypal stones were blocking Janine from telling her story in freedom. They were old filters that had followed her around her whole life.

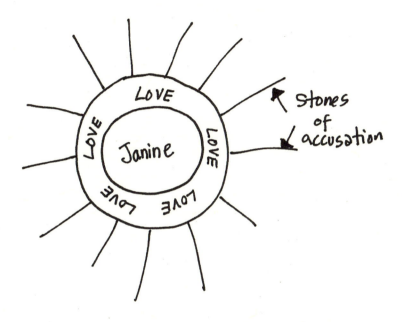

I invited Janine to imagine herself at the centre of that circle, and then I invited her to become aware of Love around her in the outer circle. Love, as Jesus did in the story, would stand between her and the stones of accusation. Love would turn to the voices of accusation. Love would respond to all those intense stones accusation. What was Love's response to those stones? What was Love's posture to those holding the stones? What happened to the stones?

We sat in silence as Janine allowed these images to fill her. Tears silently fell down her cheeks as she saw how incredibly powerful Love's energy was and the stones dissolve and became like dust. What surprised her in this experience was Love's kindness and mercy toward those accusing her. These accusers were archetypes of her critical self. There was mercy for the parts of herself that were judging herself. The stones lost their power as she became deeply aware of Love's beauty and magnificence. Light radiated from the centre of the circle and flowed out, embracing all. Love was more powerful than the fear. Love heals. Love restores. Love redeems our lives. Love rescues us from false accusations and invites truth-telling. Truth sets us free.

Love heals.
Love restores.
Love redeems our lives.
Love rescues us from false accusations and invites truth-telling.
Truth sets us free.

Next I invited her to become aware of Love turning toward her as Jesus did in the story. Once again, we entered silence as she felt aware of truth emerging toward her and addressing every single issue that the stones had represented. The purity and tenderness of Love's presence was healing and full of grace for her soul. We sat in silence as Janine internally received the truth of Love and the posture of Love toward her. As a side note, Janine does not identify with a Christian tradition; however, this story guided us into a place of understanding, truth-telling, and healing that was liberating. The inner truth of this story can still live now in our lives if we open ourselves to it.

The issue that Janine had presented at the beginning could now be held in a different light, the light of Love. Janine could speak of it tenderly, without editing herself, and dare to be true to her soul. Janine could begin to notice more clearly the Voices of Fear or the Voice of Love inside of herself. The story of the Voice of Accusation held the archetypes that helped us understand on the outside what was happening on the inside and provided an avenue of prayer and inner work that allowed Janine to know a deeper level of freedom.

This exercise can be expanded through art, collage, dream questions, poetry, and movement. It is helpful when we create something on the outside that is symbolic of the healing on the inside. In this way, our work is circular—exploring tools on the outside to free the interior and then bringing the inner work to expression in an outward form. We need symbols to help us remember truth. We so easily forget the gifts that have been given. The arts are a way for us to remember and to embody what we have received. It's important to recognize the gift and then allow it to deepen within us by holding it, reflecting upon it, and embodying it.

Healing

Healing of our psyches, our soul, our hearts is possible. It is a grace we receive. Through opening ourselves to the mystery of Love, we open to the healing that is possible for us all.

Chapter XXI

Trust—The Sacredness of it

We All Yearn for Safety

I remembering seeing her come into the retreat. She was a stately person, and you could tell she was a woman of authority, a woman who knew herself and had led others. She was around twenty years older than me and held herself with dignity and respect, yet she was coming to this retreat because she needed a safe place for her soul. She yearned to have a place to rest, to listen, to trust. I felt a little overwhelmed. *Who am I to hold space for someone beyond where I am?* I could feel a temptation toward self-doubt but then realized, as I observed her, that it was a privilege to hold space for her. I discovered I could be as a servant, one who serves a safe place for us all, a place of beauty and rest and trust no matter who we are.

We all yearn to find places of trust, a place where we can take off a role, a mask, a covering, and allow the fragile truth of our being to emerge. What is the heart looking for in seeking out places to disclose our shadows and secrets? There is a yearning in each human being, I believe, to *know oneself and to be known*. Part of ourselves becomes discovered when we feel that safety with another. When we're trusting another enough to unveil the true self, pieces of our being become unlocked, uncaged, untangled, unravelled. We emerge from hiddenness into the light of another.

Most people don't know this level of safety with other human beings, so what they're able to explore about themselves is somewhat limited. In fact, most people have known the opposite of safety—the very destruction of their tender trust. From casual indifference to blatant abuse, many people have suffered, not experiencing the gift of being deeply heard, seen, and known.

Preciousness of Trust

I believe that trust is so precious, and it can't be forced or manipulated. As I worked with hundreds of children over the years, I realized that they taught me a lot about trust. They hadn't learned the social norms yet of how to behave toward adults. Either they felt safe with you and trusted you, or they didn't. And they let it show. When a child would shyly come and sit close to me, or a twelve-year-old would disclose their fears, I realized this fragile gift of trust was being offered. I would remember when I was a child and how I longed for places of safety. I responded to these children in the best way I could, honouring their trust and bringing my full attention to them. Their lives mattered to me. Their trust mattered to me. It was like a fragile cord between us. The trust spoke silent things: I see you. I hear you. You matter.

It was like a fragile cord between us.
The trust spoke silent things;
I see you.
I hear you.
You matter.

As trust deepened over years with the music students, there was a sense of love in the music studio, a deep awareness of caring between me and the children, between the children with each other, and over time, I noticed a deepening with the parents and all the children. Trust evoked love. Love evoked community.

Trust Opens Doors

Sharon shared how being in safety, a place of trust, helped her to say things she didn't even know she needed to say. Somehow the safety evoked a trust that invited a truth-telling that was revealing, even to her own self. It created more curiosity and wonder at the inner journey she was on. It was like a door opening another door, which opened yet another door within. She shared how she experienced non-judgement as she explored her own truth-telling. This sense of safety allowed her to keep opening inner doors and know that she was still welcome. This experience was surprising to her and profoundly healing.

What else is hiding in me that I don't even know I'm covering up or yearning to express? Where is there this measure of safety in my life that I am free to explore and then reveal the truth of my being? Spiritual Direction can be one of those places of safety, a place of trust for souls to explore their inner landscape, explore their inner truth, explore the *door beyond the door*. We are invited to honour the trust given to us, to hold it tenderly. Trust is like an invisible golden thread emerging from the heart, full of beauty and fragility. We can bring sacredness to this trust and cherish it as a treasure.

Abuse of Trust

Craig was a spiritual leader and a powerful speaker with whom I became friends. I trusted he was a person of integrity, but during a conference event my intuition told me that something was amiss. A confrontation took place, and the truth revealed that Craig was full of lies and hidden ways. My trust in him as a person was completely broken. This experience was traumatic for me but taught me about the pain of shattered trust, the heartbreak when something fragile has been used or abused by another, especially by one in a position of spiritual influence and leadership. At the time of this event, I turned toward the children in the music studio with new awareness of the trust they had in me. I wanted to get on my knees and say, "I honour your trust. I will hold it as a precious gift. I will see your trust as a jewel of your soul."

Power Dynamics

When we are in a role such as a Spiritual Director, we are immediately put in a position of a power dynamic. Someone is coming to us with their trust. Often, it's the most vulnerable places within them that are needing to be met with the utmost dignity and care. This puts us in a position where we can cause great harm. Spiritual Directors are at risk of bringing damage to what is most vulnerable in another. We must be aware of this power dynamic and how it can be misused to bring more harm than healing. Harm can be caused in any number of ways: psychologically, physically, emotionally, and sexually. We are invited to walk gently as we know the sacred trust of a soul.

Abuse of Power

If there is a sexual projection happening in this power dynamic, it's not based on mutuality and therefore needs to be navigated with integrity and wisdom. At the time of this writing, the news has been released that the founder of L'Arche, Jean Vanier, abused his position of trust in Spiritual Direction and committed sexual violation with those who had come to him for spiritual care. He abused his position of power and stole something precious from the hearts that had trusted him. My heart breaks as I consider all who are impacted when one person breaks trust. Broken trust hurts the victims of such action, but it also hurts the whole community. Our integrity, or lack of it, even though hidden in our day to day lives, will yield fruit over time. Truth has a way of being revealed.

Sexuality and Spirituality

Sexuality and spirituality are both about intimacy. Spirituality is about an intimacy of the soul, a reconnection with one's own heart and a connection to Spirit. When two people share intimately about spirituality, they can experience a deep dynamic that can be projected as sexuality. If we're not integrated with our sexuality and conscious of our decisions about fidelity, moments can come that catch us off guard. However, if we are aware of sexual energy emerging, we can be open to the issue underneath the present emotion or attraction. Both director and directee can easily be hooked by projections, shadows within us needing attention. This is an opportunity for turning toward our shadows and integrating more healing.

I believe there is a deep hunger in our world for true connection, for intimacy of the heart. If a directee comes and experiences being seen or loved by the director in a pure and generous way, the directee may develop an attraction and feel a sexual pull. When suddenly they find themselves experiencing intimacy of the soul, there can be an expectation that sexuality will follow. The director in this situation is invited to notice this as a projection, a projection of the soul longing for true intimacy and relationship with the Divine. We can help to direct the projection back toward the inner journey. If they can recognize this for what it is, they can deepen their awareness and put that energy toward the spiritual work that is calling them. It takes great wisdom, firmness, and kindness to deal with these situations and to honour the dignity and beauty of each person as they find their way with their longings and passion.

As Spiritual Directors, we may notice in ourselves a sexual attraction. Sexuality is a part of our humanity and it's an energy that we must acknowledge. In this situation, we notice this within and channel this energy. This is where we need our own Spiritual Directors and therapists. What is being evoked in us? What inner shadows do we need to turn toward? What truth-telling do I need to do? How can I use this energy for good? How can I use this energy for greater integration in my own life?

Attractions of all sorts are natural and speak to the aliveness of a human being. However, when we are in a relationship with a power dynamic, there are other forces at play that must be attended to. These forces are archetypal in nature and powerful in energy. We must turn to these energies and see if the sexual energy can be used for healing or creativity. Where the sexual energy is shadowy or possessive in nature, it needs to be guided toward healing and integration with the whole self. Sexuality is not an energy to be shamed or silenced. It's a beautiful energy we carry as part of our humanity. However, it must be acknowledged and integrated in the way that holds freedom and integrity.

Relationships that hold sexual intimacy need to be based on mutuality and trust. The Spiritual Direction relationship is not a mutual relationship, and this must be understood by both parties and given utmost respect. Spiritual Direction can hold a container of *soul intimacy* that, when held with the care it deserves, offers a place for healing, growth, and beauty. However, to misuse the trust given by a directee is to abuse, harm, and violate the soul.

Our Integrity as Key to Trust
In Spiritual Direction, or any place in our lives where another is offering their trust in us, we are invited to see the preciousness of this gift. It is fragile, it is tender, it is from the inner sanctuary of a life. Our integrity, our faithfulness to our own lives, will hold the level of safety for another to be real and to expose the truth of their being. Fidelity, faithfulness in living our lives with integrity, will be our work in nurturing and honouring the trust that has been extended to us. We must understand that we are in positions of influence and power with another—power to create a sanctuary of beauty for healing and wholeness. We come as servants and companions, not as those who would abuse.

One Soul

One soul
Is a universe
When you open
The door of your heart
I see galaxies of star travel
To explore
I hear the explosions of
Waterfalls of grandeur
And the silence of
Deep-growth forests
I feel the expanse of wide-open
Vistas for me to walk gently on
For the path is your very heart
And in this moment of trust
You opened a door
And allowed me
To enter[20]

Cathy AJ Hardy

20   Cathy AJ Hardy, Love Breathes with Me (Victoria: FriesenPress, 2018), 54.

Chapter XXII

Circle of Belonging and Walking Together

The posture of Spiritual Direction is one of circle. The action of Spiritual Direction is one of walking together.

Posture of Circle

We live in a patriarchal system that has a pyramid-like structure. There's always a push to get to the top through competition, pushing, and striving. Success means being on the top of that pyramid, and only a few can arrive. To be successful, I must learn how to *conquer* a concept, *master* a strategy, and *dominate* a process.

This way of thinking impacts how we approach learning and how we face internal growth. However, internal growth and transformation do not unfold with a *conquering* mentality. The way of transformation is through being in circle and walking together.

Circle as a Symbol of Wholeness

Circles are ancient symbols of wholeness, connecting us with the natural landscape of earth, sun, and moon. We live in circular patterns of days, weeks, months, and years. Circles were used by renowned psychologist Carl Jung as a form of art meditation and dreamwork analysis to bring greater self-awareness and understanding. The mystic, Hildegarde of Bingen drew and painted many of her visions and dreams in circles, also called mandalas. First Nations communities traditionally only meet in circles, acknowledging and honouring the voices of all present. Circles invite us to have a philosophy of wholeness, of belonging, of welcome.

The Circle in Spiritual Direction

Circles are the foundation of the Soul Care work that I am dedicating my life to. Why is a circle so powerful? When we meet in circle, we honour a value system based on equality and belonging. We are face to face, and we gather knowing that each soul is significant in this meeting. Even though there are only two people gathering in Spiritual Direction, I often position the furniture and images in the room so there is a sense of circle, a sense that we are *at the table of belonging* together. This construct places the director in a position of humility and equality of value with the directee. For retreats and larger gatherings, my intention is always to create a sense of circle as we gather in community. Even though unspoken, a circle communicates subconscious messages of connection and togetherness.

Growth as Circular/Spiral

Spiritual growth, or inner personal growth, is often circular in nature. Transformation isn't a linear line forward, an object to be attained or conquered. It's more like a *spiral of change* or a pathway along a labyrinth. Growth invites us to circle back around and go deeper and higher, much like the growth of a tree. The inner lines of a tree trunk show this spectacular circular growth that propels the tree both farther into the earth and farther into the sky. This model of growth is important to ponder in light of Spiritual Direction.

Many people get frustrated when they haven't *arrived*, or when they feel they're circling back to an old issue. They're frustrated because they're operating out of a pyramid mentality that holds the belief, "once conquered, always conquered." Real growth is like a slow expansion, like stepping out into new landscape, walking around, and then returning to a place of safety. Then one walks around again and stays a while before returning. Over and over, one must expand enough until one can remain in the new territory. Then there will be an invitation for growth into a larger landscape. Back and forth. Deeper into the earth. Higher into the sky. A spiral of growth. This kind of growth is truly transformative ... and it is slow.

Growth, a Slow Journey

How disappointing to many that this is a slow journey! "Perhaps I'll take this course and *arrive!* Perhaps I'll meditate for three weeks and become enlightened. Can you just tell me how to transform?" These comments I've heard over the years speak to our idea of *attaining* transformation—that growth is something we can *buy or achieve.* But this kind of inner growth doesn't work with the Western idea of consumerism. Transformation is slow ... and it's a process of choosing again and again to yield, surrender, trust, and rest, opening the heart to beauty, spaciousness, tenderness, and mercy.

> *Transformation is slow...*
> *and it's a process*
> *of choosing again and again*
> *to yield,*
> *surrender, trust, and rest,*
> *opening the heart to*
> *beauty, spaciousness,*
> *tenderness,*
> *and mercy.*

Transformation is slow because the soul journey invites us to follow another rhythm than that of our culture: the rhythm of the heart, the rhythm of the soul. What if one truth takes a decade to absorb? What if a paradigm shift is a slow reconstruction over twenty years? Can we have patience for ourselves? For others? This slow journey of transformation happens over time, over a long walk, one we never finish. This way of walking becomes a *way of life*, not a course we take.

This Journey Is a Walk

I like to think of this soul journey as a walk, a slow steady walk into deeper Love, toward wholeness and freedom. We learn more from the modelling of others than from ingesting information. When I walk with you, we take time to walk and talk through things together. As we walk by this tree, it reminds us of a story, and we sit there and chat for a while. As we walk by a stream, it evokes another conversation. We set up camp for the night, and we sit in darkness with each other. Then we become aware of the dawn and we set out once again.

Spiritual Direction is the art of walking with another—the slow walk through life's passages and learning through walking *with*. Walking with another who has walked this trail many times gives me comfort, and I learn from observation. I notice how they are aware of the new buds on the tree. I notice how they navigate the stream as we cross over. I notice how they set up the tent as we enter darkness. I notice how they're not afraid of the darkness and know how to be in it instead of resist it. I notice how they're comfortable with silence and have patience to wait for dawn. I notice how they're at peace with the ebb and flow of journey. The wise guides I have known have taught me how to walk so that I can now walk with others in this beautiful, but slow, gentle journey.

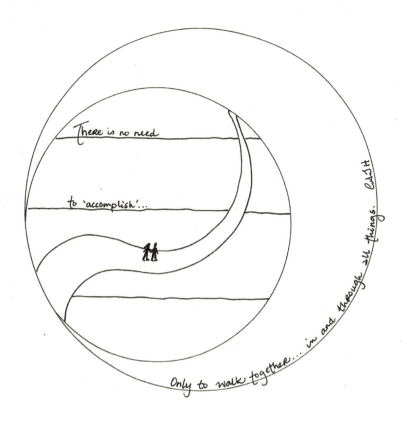

There is no need

to 'accomplish'...

Only to walk together... in and through all things. CJSH

Walking Together

The beautiful art of Spiritual Direction is a way of walking together through life. It is a sense of companionship through the ebb and flow of life, a soul friendship where one can lean into presence and remember what is true. The truth of one's being is alive in each person but most people fall into forgetting who they are and are pulled out of themselves into fear and control. The long journey of Spiritual Direction allows us to keep falling back into the *rhythm of knowing the truth of our souls*. Spiritual Direction is a gift guiding our lives toward being re-membered, re-turned, and re-called home.

Spiritual Direction
is a gift guiding our lives
toward
being re-membered,
re-turned,
and re-called
home.

A Circle—A Space to be Recalled, Returned, Remembered

Re-membered

Gertrud Muller Nelson in her book *Here All Dwell Free*, shares the old story of how a shaman would become initiated.[21] The elder shamans would take the younger member and "dis-member" them to the ends of the earth for a long night. In the morning, they would *re-member* the parts and return them to wholeness. There was an understanding that to become a shaman, one needed to understand the healing journey, the path from being fractured and re-membered into wholeness.

In Spiritual Direction, we open up a container and, even though nothing may be said about healing per se, it happens. There is a *re-membering* of the parts that are fractured within us as they are seen and witnessed, brought to Love, held in grace.

Re-turned

It's powerful to think of the significance of return. What does it mean to return home? Home to our souls? Home to our integrity? Many of us have been disconnected from ourselves and have betrayed our own hearts. Being returned is the invitation to re-turn and face our lives and come home to the truth within.

....

21   Gertrud Mueller Nelson, Here All Dwell Free (New York: Doubleday, 1991), 124.

Taking time for inner work creates a space that invites us to move from a posture of looking outwards for home and return to the inner wellsprings that are there for us all. Many of us are looking outwards for fulfillment, meaning, purpose, and satisfaction. What if we returned home and found those things within? Finding home within, through learning to draw from the wellsprings of life, allows us to live from the inside out, from a place of inner abundance and generosity to those around us. Instead of grasping, we are giving. Instead of clinging, we are creating. Instead of pining, we are providing.

Finding home within,
through learning to draw from the wellsprings of life,
allows us to live from the inside out,
from a place of inner abundance and generosity to those around us.

Jesus talked about this inner wellspring, but I haven't met very many people who are living from this reality. Brother Roger of Taizé has been a role model for my life in this regard. He often referred in his writings to living from the inner wellspring. His face was radiant, and I recognized in him someone who was congruent with themselves. He wasn't speaking religious jargon but living from an inner knowing. I became curious and longed for what I saw and heard in him. Brother Roger inspired me on the path of silence, of listening, of slowing down, of being attentive, of letting go. All of these things, over time, opened my heart to receive what is within us all.

When I am empty and when I have given away all my heart holds, it's time for stillness, for rest of the heart, for receiving and dropping deep down into silence. It is here that I can again receive what my soul needs. Prayer, in this place, is a time of communion, a filling of the cup, an eating of the bread, a restoration of the mind and body. Silence is a way to *return* over and over and over. We are invited to *live* from this place of return and invite others to join us in this way of being.

Instead of grasping, we are giving.
Instead of clinging, we are creating.
Instead of pining, we are providing.

Re-called

I believe in the significance of names and the meaning of names. Being re-called, as I see it, is living out from truth how Love names us. I used to struggle with my own name, Cathy. It means "pure one," and the implications that I felt growing up were for me to live in a moral straightjacket. When I began to explore the meaning of pure, I realized that purity is about finding the essence of the thing. When alcohol is purified, it has gone through a refining process and becomes clear and potent. Purity became a beautiful word about living out of the *essence* of my true self with the false self being burned away. I began to love my name and become curious about all of my names. What were my names teaching me? What were they calling me to be? In many myths and legends as well as Gospel stories, the naming of someone is a powerful proclamation of who they are. How are we being re-called to our true names?

We all experience being labelled at different moments of our lives— false names that have put us in a box, shamed us, or silenced us. These false names can be like poison, influencing how we see ourselves and how we move through the world. Labels take us away from our essence, but Love guides us to know the inheritance of our truth.

As I struggled with the labels I experienced from a difficult situation, I walked to an open field and shouted to the sky: "Who do you say that I am?" This is the same question that Jesus asked his friends. But now I wanted to ask it too. I wanted to know, I wanted to really know, how does the Living Presence name me? What is the truth of my name? What am I called? My desire in that moment was to orient myself to being re-called so I could dare to live from the fullness of truth rather than the shadow places of distortion.

What I experienced in that moment out in the field surprised me greatly. The words I heard overwhelmed me with beauty. I wrote them down and then hid them for a year. It was too much to absorb. Could I dare to receive such goodness? Could I dare to say these words out loud? Could I dare to live from this place of being re-called? Those words became a song which I then dared, after a year, to sing. To my great surprise, as I sang these words for a group of friends for the first time, I was met with silence and tears flowing down many cheeks. These words resonated with the hearts present. We *all* needed to be re-called. We all needed to know the truth of our being.

We're invited over and over again to *live from our true names*, the words of truth that Love is singing over us. Our energy, our presence, our vitality is directly affiliated with this alignment of truth. How we are present to others flows from knowing our names and living out of the reality of how Love sees us.

The Gift of Offering Blessing

When we name others in blessing it can be so deeply restorative and healing. Sometimes I wonder what would happen if we dared to speak out blessing more often—words of being re-called, re-turned, re-membered. Listening to another, seeing another, valuing another are ways of blessing that heal the soul. Daring to speak out words of life is another profound gift we can offer—words of truth, words of life, words that ignite the heart to live.

Coming Home

Perhaps the image of coming home is a beautiful way to understand the symbolism of circle. As Sue Monk Kidd writes: "The image of coming home is a powerful, archetypal symbol for returning to one's deepest self, to the soul. To come home is to return to the place of inner origin, that original imprint of God within. Therefore, coming home fills us with a sense of being in the right place, a sense of deep spiritual belonging."[22]

22   Sue Monk Kidd, When the Heart Waits (New York: HarperCollins, 1990), 89.

Chapter XXIII

Discernment Process and Threshold Crossings

One of the great gifts that Spiritual Direction offers is a sacred place to process discernment during times of transition. Life is an ever-unfolding movement of decisions and change. We often experience a sense of pressure to make large life decisions too quickly and to move on to a new reality that is happening in our lives. Times of discernment and times of crossing a threshold are sacred and often need a sense of spaciousness to fully honour the reality of what is happening.

Threshold Crossings

John O'Donohue, the great Celtic author and poet, writes about the sacredness of crossing a threshold, a place of transition in one's life. John's work in his book, *To Bless the Space Between Us,*[23] caused me to ponder the significance of moments of transition and wonder how we can honour these seasons in meaningful ways. A threshold is a place of crossing, a space in between one reality and another.

Some of the recent threshold moments in my own life have been: when my mother died, when my children moved out of the house, when I became a single woman again through my divorce, and when I retired from teaching music and entered Soul Care work full-time.

---

23   John O'Donohue, To Bless the Space Between Us (New York: Doubleday, 2008), 47

When I completed teaching music after thirty-six years, I experienced many conflicting emotions. There was a sadness in letting go of the beauty of relationships that had been a rhythm in my life for many years. Things wouldn't be the same, and I wasn't sure what my new rhythms would feel like. I also experienced joy because there was a knowing that I was answering a ten-year call, and I was finally saying a full *yes*. At the same time, I was afraid because I didn't know if I could financially support myself, and I wondered what might happen. My body fell apart shortly after my retirement. Some physical issues that had plagued me in mild ways for years came rushing into the scene, causing me to stop in many ways.

Permission to Give Myself Time

My health became a major concern, and I saw many health care workers who all offered me a piece to the puzzle of my restoration. But an awareness grew in me that I was in a time of threshold, an *in between time* of a huge vocational shift. I needed to allow a year of adjustment mentally, emotionally, physically, and spiritually. Pushing myself to enter this new life without taking time to grieve and let go of the old was expecting too much of myself. Allowing my body to fall apart was a way to give permission to myself to be in transition, threshold, change. Eventually, over many months, answers did come for my health. But I began to hold those answers in the light of being in gentle transition, giving myself time.

Through this experience, I realized what pressure there is to move quickly from one thing to another in our culture whether it be grief, change, or losses of different kinds. Even the simple reality of *naming* this time of transition as *threshold,* a doorway between a before and after, has allowed myself and others to take a deep breath and just *be* with the feelings and processes that arise with change.

We are invited to honour the seasons of threshold and allow the many conflicting emotions that come with these sacred times in our lives. Whatever the transition is, it means a significant moment in our lives that is worth taking time to acknowledge. Even though we may be thrilled at the change we're experiencing, we may need to honour the beauty of what we had before and grieve that it is no longer in our hands. Just like a child moving out of the house, we need to hold the pictures, walk into the bedrooms, and linger with the memories even as we celebrate the new steps in their lives.

Questions for the Time of Threshold

To honour this time of change, I've developed some questions that may be helpful for those in this place of threshold. To write and express our truth is a way of validating our experiences. It also allows curiosity and creativity to emerge in the space we find ourselves.

- *As I look back at what is now closing or complete, what am I grateful for?*
- *What were some of the consolations and desolations I experienced?*
- *What were some of my greatest learnings?*
- *What are some of the memories I will cherish?*
- *What still feels raw or painful that I need to turn toward with compassion?*
- *What are some ways I can do this? On my own or with another?*
- *Where have I experienced growth in my life because of this past situation/relationship?*
- *What do I want to carry forward?*
- *What do I want to release?*
- *Where do I stand now?*
- *What feels uncertain and confusing in this threshold time?*
- *What feels restful and calm?*
- *What am I afraid of?*
- *What are some of the things I know for sure as I look forward?*
- *What am I proud of in my journey?*

- *What are the longings I am aware of as I take time for stillness?*
- *Where do I feel compelled to push or strive instead of wait?*
- *What is the invitation I become aware of as I take time for silence?*

Discernment

The process of discernment is another threshold experience that is often rushed. Many people come into Spiritual Direction when they are faced with huge decisions about their next step. Most feel a pressure to figure this out in a timely manner. I invite them into a sense of spaciousness, a *process* of discernment. The Ignatian tradition saw the process of discernment in decision making as a very sacred time. Here are some questions to consider if entering discernment.

- *What if we take three months to hold a position of not-knowing? (or another length of time)*
- *What if we write down all the questions that this discernment issue is creating?*
- *What if we sit with the tension?*
- *Who are three people who love me and hold wisdom that I could process this decision with?*
- *What if we listen to the body as we explore various options?*
- *What are the pushes and pulls that one inwardly feels in this decision?*
- *What is the voice of Wisdom within that emerges over time?*

Listening to Three Energy Centres

Being in discernment is to allow one to access all three intelligence centres: the body, the mind, the heart. Making big decisions about one's life isn't something to only analyze intellectually. We enter a posture of being attentive to many small things that are arising within. It may be hard to put our finger on all of the subtle places of awareness that may develop, and that is why taking time is so vital in making decisions that are *congruent* with the soul.

Healthy feminine consciousness, the inner place of intuition and soulful awareness, lives in all of us. However, it's the aspect in our culture that has been largely over-run. To be integrated, we need to listen to the feminine within, which often takes more time, is more subtle, and is connected to awareness in our bodies. We have over-valued some unhealthy masculine energies in our society that value what we can measure, what we can prove, what we can attain. The work of slowing down and listening is about healing the silenced feminine, restoring the masculine, and bringing a beautiful union of wholeness into our lives. This reality can be practiced as we enter times of discernment.

Listening to facts and reason *and* holding space for the body and intuition without rushing is a powerful way to learn a balance between the radiant feminine and the resilient masculine in each of us.

- *What are the facts around this decision, the details that would impact me if I move one way or another?*
- *What are the subtle emotions of this decision, the fears, and the hopes?*
- *What is my gut sense about this decision?*
- *Where do I feel tension or release in my body as I consider saying yes or no?*

Spiritual Direction is a beautiful container
for allowing spaciousness
in the tension
of the unknown.

Sacred Seasons

Crossing a threshold and taking time for discernment are sacred seasons in our lives worth noticing and honouring with spaciousness and dignity. Spiritual Direction is a beautiful container for allowing spaciousness in the tension of the unknown. These times of process can be held in love, patience, and kindness.

Surrender

Pause
Wait
Not sure of where to
place my step
Pause
Wait
I've never travelled here before

More uncertainty
Than clarity to my thoughts
All I have
Are questions
And my questions
Are my prayer

My hands are reaching
For something I can grasp

My feet are yearning
For a firm
Foundation

In all unknowing
I
am
here

I place my heart
in the light of the sun
I place my hands
on the quest of my heart
I place my feet
in the path of this quest
And
Surrender[24]

Cathy AJ Hardy

24 Cathy AJ Hardy, Love Breathes with Me (Victoria: FriesenPress, 2018), 14.

Chapter XXIV

Integration—Healing Inner Masculine and Feminine Energies

Masculine and Feminine Energies

We are complex beings. Carl Jung, Swiss psychiatrist and psycho-analyst, explored the inner landscape of the human psyche in ground breaking ways. One of the breakthroughs in Western psychology Jung came to discover is that we all, as human beings, carry opposing inner energies, what he called the anima and the animus. This was a similar understanding to what ancient Chinese philosophy called yin and yang. With Jung's language, the anima stood for the feminine energy, and the animus for the masculine energy. As humans, we carry these magnetic opposing energies. These energies are a part of our inner reality, no matter what gender we identify with. Part of our work is to bring these energies into healing, wholeness, and, most of all, relationship and integration with one another.

Masculine Energy

An integrated and healed masculine energy feels like presence, a still mountain. It holds clarity and deep knowing; it is unhurried, rooted, grounded, aware, and awake. To be in the company of the healed and whole masculine is to experience stillness, awareness, calm, and intention.

An unhealed masculine energy feels like zest with no direction and spinning tires. It seeks control over others, domination, and exploitation. It is ego-driven. This energy values measurement against one another, unhealthy competition, and pushing to the top of the pyramid no matter how much carnage. It's not a safe energy to be around as it's full of destructive chaos and confusion.

Healing the Masculine

How do we heal the masculine energy? Through stillness, finding mindfulness of breath and body. By valuing life itself, the masculine discovers *presence*. The masculine energy within needs to slow down and become conscious, thus recognizing meaning in *being*. When the masculine finds inner presence, there is an *awareness* of value, purpose, integrity, and awake-ness. Stillness and silence become teachers for the masculine and guide this inner energy toward standing with an inner posture of clarity and truth. The masculine moves from a place of frenzied activity to a place of still strength. When the masculine energy heals, it moves from aimless action to purposeful presence. It is transformed from dominating oppression to soulful service.

> *When the masculine energy heals,*
> *it moves from aimless action*
> *to purposeful presence.*

Our Culture

Our culture is largely driven by an unhealthy dominating masculine energy— resulting in much action without meaning or purpose. This energy has valued ideas over human lives, goods over nature, dominance over equality. We can see this everywhere we turn. Our governments, churches, institutions, and work places are filled with this energy, and it impacts and harms all of us, whatever gender we identify with.

Feminine Energy

Part of the healing of the soul is to rediscover the inner feminine energy. This has been so deeply silenced and diminished by the culture at large that we don't even know this aspect of ourselves. But if we learn to pay attention, this feminine energy longs to be awakened and restored to life. What is the feminine? It's the place in all of us of our *deepest intuitive knowing*. You know, that moment when you walk into a room and you have a sense about something? The inner awareness that is hard to put your finger on and find words for, but you *just know*? The aspect inside that feels murky, confusing, and mystifying. The aspect inside that also is wise, discerning, and astute. The feminine is deeply connected to our bodies. We often have a hunch or a gut sense; however, these elements, so powerful and insightful, are easily laughed at, dismissed, and thrown out by the culture at large. When the feminine energy awakens and heals, it's the place from which we create, flow, birth, imagine, delight, wonder, and dance.

Silenced and Stagnated Feminine

When an aspect of ourselves, a person, or a people group has been silenced or exploited, a reaction can occur in all sorts of ways. Sometimes a deep depression or a turning to addiction is a way to endure. Sometimes the oppressed will befriend the oppressor in hopes of being seen or acknowledged, only to realize they're being used. Sometimes a wild rage will erupt, and death is even embraced to speak out a truth. The suppressed feminine, within all of us, lurks as a shadow of moodiness, depression, addiction, anger, and more.

When the feminine energy is lost and silenced, there is a *stagnation* of energy within. We feel this physically. We lose our flow, our creative juice, our joy, our sense of aliveness. It's vital to notice when we see these signs in ourselves because it means that the feminine archetype within needs attention. This energy is longing for reconnection. But how?

Healing the Feminine

How does the feminine energy heal? The feminine aspect within needs to be nurtured, seen, listened to, acknowledged, valued, and cherished. When we really come home to ourselves, we come to face that inner knowing and are invited to become friends with our souls. And the way to see, listen, acknowledge, value, and cherish the feminine within is through listening to the deepest aspects of ourselves, shadows and all. Some say that the masculine energy is like being in the sun, as it holds the aspects of life that are measurable and obvious. However, the feminine nature in us is like being in the light of the moon. This is the inner space within that takes moves slowly and requires patience, trust, and spaciousness.

We need to learn to *be with ourselves* and know ourselves. When we truly listen to our hearts, we will notice an unblocking of energy. This takes constant courage, as sometimes we'd rather not listen to what our hearts have to say! Awakening the feminine can be messy, as our hearts always want to tell us the truth. However, when we listen to the truth of our lives, this heals something so utterly deep within. When the feminine heals, she *rises* and *births* creativity, movement, life.

When the feminine energy heals, it moves from *blocked breath to radiant flow*. It transforms from oppressed silence to creative expression. There is a sense of vitality, released energy, and illumination. When the feminine is back to life, we will know *flowing energy*. She moves from a place of stagnation to a place of movement, life, and creativity! The feminine longs to birth new realities and is the *veriditas* (greening energy described by Hildegarde von Bingen) within, always generative.

The Integration

Integration is the union of the *flow* of the feminine with the *presence* of the masculine. *Presenced action* becomes the integrated reality. Purposeful energy, intentional movement, soul-filled creativity, vitality, and clarity become the fruit of the healed masculine and feminine energies within.

Presenced action
becomes the integrated reality.
Integration is about radiant energy
flowing from integrity.

The healed feminine can bring healing to the unhealed masculine energy within through being attentive to deep knowing in the body and soul. The healed masculine heals the feminine by holding space, being fully present, and by conscious awareness. These energies have potential to heal each other, and when they do, it allows a profound inner partnership. The masculine energy we all carry needs *purpose and direction*. When the inner knowing, the feminine energy, knows what it knows and is listened to, the masculine energy can *serve that knowing* and find the deepest sense of vitality, purpose, and strength. Suddenly, movement isn't aimless but is filled with meaning and purpose. Action isn't based in power-over but in service.

Integration is about bringing *presence in service to the inner knowing*. Integration is about *radiant energy flowing from integrity*. Power-filled action arises from a place of *essence* rather than domination. The integration of the two energies in one person brings life *for the whole community*, not only the individual. This changes everything.

Spiritual Direction
The journey of healing the feminine and masculine energies is one of profound transformation. When a life finds meaning and purpose, everything looks different. When a life feels listened to and is able to take action from that deep knowing, a sense of flow and vitality emerges that creates an actual glow on the human face. One begins to actually live the life they were yearning for instead of surviving. Integration of

the inner person impacts the world, because we have found what made us come alive. A healed soul brings healing to the world.

Through Spiritual Direction, our listening helps others listen to themselves, perhaps for the first time. This is the beginning of healing and integrating the masculine and feminine energies within.

You are invited to open
To listen again to the
Inner Knowing
To see again the richness
Of your heart
To turn again to your dear heart
And cherish
The preciousness
Of your life.
Feel the Feminine Rise.
You are invited to breathe
To feel the strength of your vitality
To feel the depths of your Presence
To know the roots
of your tree
To sink in Silence
Feel the Masculine Stand
You are invited to unite
The Stillness with the Flow
The Presence with the Knowing
The Standing with the Creating
Integration
Presenced Action
Embodied Grace

Cathy AJ Hardy

Chapter XXV

Partnership—Service from the Tent

Image of the Tent

Several years before this writing, I saw an image in my mind that has stayed with me, supporting me when I've been weary. I was standing at the front of a tent, and there was a long line of people coming to this tent for care. My hands were empty, my heart overwhelmed, as I stood looking at the vast expanse of need before me.

Be Attentive and Open up to the Gifts

As the first person came forward in the line, I realized the tent was expanding behind me; an eternal storehouse of knowledge, wisdom, insight, and courage. This tent was filled with endless shelves and limitless rooms. I became aware of an invitation to meet each person and simply listen to what was happening in their lives. Then I was to become aware that this storehouse of wisdom and blessing was available for all we would need. I could be attentive to what was being brought forward from the tent. I didn't have to *do* anything except *be present* to each one and open up to the gifts that were waiting for them.

This image has helped me countless times when I've been fatigued and greatly aware of my lack. It's not my skill, wisdom, or knowledge that ultimately helps me as a Spiritual Director. It's the posture of open hands and a listening heart that allows for a greater mystery to unfold and the gifts from the tent to come forward.

Partnership

As I sit with the image of being at the front of the tent, there is a sense of partnership with Wisdom. Love is flowing through me, and I am a channel for Love. Spiritual Direction, for me, is about this beautiful partnership with the Living Presence. In this partnership, I have the blessing of being available to souls on the journey. This is a great privilege and a part of my life I am deeply grateful for.

> *It is not my skill, wisdom, or knowledge*
> *that helps me most as a Spiritual Director.*
> *It is the posture*
> *of open hands*
> *and a listening heart*
> *that allows for a greater mystery to unfold and*
> *the gifts from the tent*
> *to come forward.*

After I completed writing this text, I came across the writings of Hildegarde von Bingen, mystic saint and Doctor of the Catholic Church.[25] To my surprise, I found out that she also wrote of a tent, the tent of Wisdom that our life and work flows from. Perhaps this image of service from the tent has lived in other hearts as well. May we know the generative and abundant energy that comes from Wisdom, the source Hidegarde called greening energy, *veriditas*, the life-flow that is creative, generative, and the Source of all things.

---

25   Matthew Fox, Hildegard of Bingen (Vancouver: Namaste Publishing, 2012), xxii.

Conclusion and Blessing

There is no formula for being a Spiritual Director. In fact, each one I have encountered has offered something unique and beautiful. I believe that the qualities of a Spiritual Director are not about having a certain personality type or manner, but about essence. When one is *authentically themselves*, at rest in their souls, a healing space is offered for anyone in their presence. If we are inwardly at rest, we are able to hold space for another with great attentiveness and listening.

We need all kinds of Spiritual Directors, Holy Listeners, Companions on the Way. The invitation is to be a Loving Presence from the *truth of your own life*, the beauty of your soul. We are not meant to contort ourselves into one cookie cutter shape, but to radiate from the inner wellsprings the *essence* of beauty that each of us carries. This offers a way of liberty and freedom for each of us to explore.

> *The invitation is to be a Loving Presence*
> *from the truth of your own life,*
> *the beauty of your soul.*

In closing, I'd like to share with you some beautiful words from Denise that reflect her journey with Spiritual Direction:

"I have been receiving Spiritual Direction for the past five years. I am learning that it is a very deliberate, thoughtful, sometimes arduous journey. I have to say, the walk is very slow—much slower than I would have expected or wanted in the beginning. I have always been drawn to doing things to make my life better ... and the quicker the better. This

has not been my experience with Spiritual Direction. I used to bring my lists of the things that I wanted to fix, to correct within myself or others. I no longer do this. It's an arbitrary exercise, because usually I'm led in a completely different direction. Led. That's the difference. Led to listen. To watch. To pay attention to my body, my longings, my emotions, and to not fix but to just notice and to hold.

I have begun to accept the process and to trust that Love—beautiful Love—is already doing what needs to be done in me and with me. Together. Not separate, not ever.

I have begun to notice a love for myself growing inside. Little things like when I feel angry, I don't push it down and away but allow space and begin to ask questions. To allow myself to be, to fill space, to feel. There isn't a particular situation when I remember this "happening" for me. It was one day a thought, another day ... a different choice, another day ... a peace where there wasn't before. Little by little my roots were growing deeper into Love, deeply connecting to my Source, feeling home in a way I've never felt before. I began to heal. Really heal.

In our last spiritual direction together, I asked Cathy the age-old question, the great qualifier: 'Aren't I supposed to serve the world in some way?' Essentially, 'Shouldn't I be doing more?'

'More?' she asked. 'More than being who you were created to be? More than letting yourself be healed by Love and moving from that place? More than being home in yourself and serving Love and the world from that place? Your wholeness heals the world.'

When I nurture my roots, when I let Love heal me and move from that place, it is the greatest service that I can bring to the world. When I walk where I cannot see, trusting the way. When I walk my walk alone, leaning into Love. When I leave behind the voices that are not for me, I am in fidelity to Love—and to myself—and from that place, Love only knows what is possible."

Blessing

It is my hope that this text has been an encouragement to you in your pursuit of learning about Spiritual Direction. With any subject, the conversation is never complete. There is always more to explore and to learn. However, I hope that some of this writing has been helpful for you in this particular time of your reading.

I'd like to close this book with a blessing from my heart to yours:

May you be blessed by knowing your name.
May you be blessed by knowing your value.
May you be blessed by knowing your beauty.
May you discern the path before you with joy and rest.
May you deepen into silence.
May you deepen into trust.
May you deepen into the Gaze of Love.
May you deepen into receiving from the inner wellsprings.
May you stand in the truth of your presence.
May you flow with the wild river of Love.
May you expand into your true nature.
May you blossom into your fullness.
May you be recalled, returned, remembered
To the beauty of your soul
And union with Love.

Gratitude and Acknowledgements

Two women who shaped my life beyond what I could have ever imagined have my heart of gratitude. Joy and Doreen, your love is imprinted on my heart and has changed the landscape of my life; I dedicate this text to you. Forever grateful. One day, may you catch a glimpse of the fruit of your love.

Walt and Elsie Goerzen: Elsie, you have been my biggest cheerleader with this text, spurring me on and listening to my heart along the way. I feel your love; I know your friendship. You are an inspiration to me, and I'm delighted to call you friend. Walt, your time and energy with the details of this text will not be forgotten. I am grateful for your perspective, insight, and diligence in guiding me to work through the editing process. Love you both.

To Kerry Wilson, my editor at FriesenPress, thank you for your support and encouragement. I greatly appreciate all you have done for me! For all the other staff at FriesenPress that made this book possible, thank you.

To the small circle of 2020 Haden graduates I mentored—the circle of women who I began to write this for, before I understood I was writing a book. Thank you for inspiring me to share my heart with you. Thank you for singing with me and becoming ignited with the Fire: Elise, Chris, Beth, Allie, Karen, Jan, and Janice.

To the Soul Care Community birthed in the Fraser Valley of BC, Canada and now growing beyond. You inspire me to live fully. I am so grateful to walk together. You know who you are, and you are many. I'm grateful for you.

Printed in Canada